Parasites

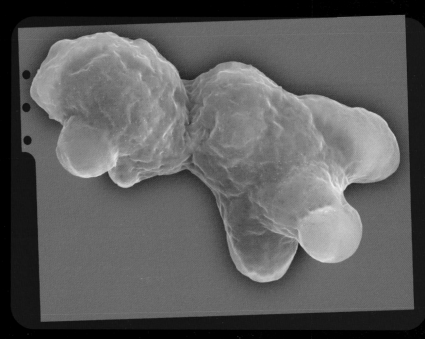

sites

Latching On to a Free Lunch

Paul Fleisher

 Twenty-First Century Books ■ Minneapolis

In recognition of the service of public health workers everywhere, including my mother, Tresa Fleisher, who spent many years making sure the citizens of Hartford County kept their hands and workplaces clean.

The author would like to express his appreciation to Edward O. Wilson, Bert Hölldobler, Carl Zimmer, and Paul Ewald, whose writings first piqued his curiosity about parasites, and to Joelle Riley, for her editorial guidance.

Twenty-First Century Books
A division of Lerner Publishing Group
241 First Avenue North
Minneapolis, Minnesota 55401 U.S.A.

Website address: www.lernerbooks.com

Library of Congress Cataloging-in-Publication Data

Fleisher, Paul.
     Parasites : latching on to a free lunch / by Paul Fleisher.
        p.   cm. — (Discovery!)
     Includes bibliographical references and index.
     ISBN-13: 978–0–8225–3415–0 (lib. bdg. : alk. paper)
     ISBN-10: 0–8225–3415–0 (lib. bdg. : alk. paper)
     1. Parasites—Juvenile literature. I. Title. II. Series: Discovery! (Lerner Publications
Company)
QL757.F55 2006
578.6'5—dc22   2005010521

Manufactured in the United States of America
1 2 3 4 5 6 – BP – 11 10 09 08 07 06

CONTENTS

Chapter One

PARASITES ALL AROUND US

Look at the living world around you. Squirrels scramble up a tree. Birds perch in the branches. Bees and butterflies fly from flower to flower. Maybe a rabbit is nibbling clover in the backyard. What could be simpler? But look again. Almost every creature you see—plant or animal—is an unwilling host to several different kinds of parasite.

Now look in the mirror. You probably have company too. You may not feel a thing, but there's a good chance you are hosting a few unwanted guests. There may be tiny mites living in your hair or a fungus growing on the skin between your toes. Perhaps there are amoebas living in your gums or a few worms colonizing your intestines.

Our world is swarming with parasites. Most parasites are small. They often live hidden inside other creatures, so we may not take much notice of them. When we study the natural world, free-living species such as wolves, crickets, palm trees, and sharks get most of our attention. But parasites' life histories are truly amazing. They are highly specialized and complex. It is impossible to fully understand our living world without understanding the lives of parasites.

In this book, you'll meet dozens of different parasites. They come from all branches of our living world—fungi, plants, animals, and protists (single-celled organisms that are neither plants

This scanning electron micrograph image gives an up close look at a head louse clinging to human hair. Lice are parasites that feed on the blood of their hosts.

nor animals). They have some of the most incredible life cycles you've ever heard of. You'll discover that although we rarely see them, parasites play a big part in the story of life on Earth.

What Is a Parasite?

A parasite is an organism that lives in or on another organism, called the host, and gets its nutrients directly from it. Ordinarily, a parasite lives with its host for an extended period of time. It usually causes damage to the host without killing it directly. Creatures that do not live as parasites are called free-living species.

A few parasites may already be familiar to you. You may have heard of tapeworms or pinworms, which live in the intestines of animals and humans. You probably know about the fleas, lice, and ticks that often plague our pets and may bite us too. The sprig of mistletoe hanging above the door at Christmastime comes from a parasitic plant. But those few examples are just the beginning of a very long list.

Just about every kind of free-living animal and plant has several parasitic species that live on it. There are more parasites on Earth than free-living species. Some parasites even have their own parasites, called hyperparasites. For example, fleas and lice live as parasites on a dog or cat. But the fleas themselves may be infected with tiny worms.

It's not always easy to decide whether an organism is a parasite. A cow eats grass. Is the cow a grass parasite? Biologists would say no. Humans raise cows for milk. We harvest the milk that a cow would otherwise feed to her calf. Are we parasites of cows? Again, biologists would say no.

Not every relationship between animals is so simple. A mosquito lands on an animal, drinks its blood, and flies away to lay its eggs in a nearby puddle. Is the mosquito a parasite? How about a louse, which lives on an animal's skin, drinks its blood, and then lays eggs in the animal's hair?

Lice are considered parasites. They live on, as well as feed on, their host. But biologists call mosquitoes micropredators, not parasites. Predators are creatures that attack and feed on other animals. Micropredators are simply tiny predators that feed on others without killing them.

Viruses and bacteria certainly live parasitic lives. They survive inside other creatures and take nutrients from them to grow and reproduce. But by tradition, most biologists don't classify them as parasites either.

LIVING TOGETHER

Different kinds of plants and animals often live in close connection with one another. The relationship between two different species that live together and interact with one another is called symbiosis. Biologists divide symbiosis into several different categories.

Mutualism is one type of symbiosis. Both partners benefit from a mutual relationship. For example, cleaner shrimp on a coral reef have a mutual relationship with many kinds of fish. At special "cleaning stations," large fish open their mouths and allow the cleaner shrimp to remove parasites and bits of food from their teeth and gills. The shrimp get a meal, and the fish get a cleaning that keeps them healthy.

Commensalism is another type of symbiosis. Only one of the two creatures seems to benefit in a commensal relationship. The other is neither helped nor harmed. The pea crab and the oyster have a commensal relationship. Small, soft-bodied pea crabs live inside mollusks such as oysters, clams, and mussels. The crabs

A cleaner shrimp gets a meal, while a moray eel gets a cleaning. Since both creatures benefit, their symbiotic relationship is known as mutualism.

are protected by the stony shells of the mollusks. They gather food from the water that the mollusks draw into their shells. The mollusks don't seem to gain anything by sharing their shells with the crabs, but they don't suffer any harm either.

Another relationship between species is predation. A predator, such as a panther, kills and eats its prey. Clearly only one of the organisms benefits from this relationship.

Finally, there's parasitism. A parasite uses its host organism for both food and habitat. It attaches itself to its host and feeds for days, weeks, or even years. Parasites that live within the body of a host are called endoparasites. Those that live on the outside—on the skin or hair, for example—are called ectoparasites. A parasite may weaken its host and shorten its life, but most don't kill the host outright. Parasites that do kill their hosts as part of their life cycle are classified as parasitoids.

The life cycles of parasites are often very complex. Many parasites have two or three different hosts during their lives. The species that hosts a parasite's adult, reproductive stage is called its definitive host. The hosts for its juvenile stages are known as intermediate hosts. Liver flukes are parasitic worms that spend their adult lives in the liver of a sheep. As juveniles they live in the bodies of freshwater snails. The snails are the flukes' intermediate host. Sheep are its definitive host.

A host that transmits parasites from one organism to another is called a vector. Mosquitoes are vectors that transmit the parasite that causes malaria. A mosquito bites someone infected with malaria and takes in malaria parasites with its blood meal. When the mosquito later bites another person, malaria parasites are passed on to the new host.

Many free-living creatures are quite adaptable when it comes to what they eat. A bobcat might prefer to hunt rabbits, but many other kinds of prey will do. The bobcat can survive perfectly well on squirrels or frogs or quail. Similarly, a deer can eat many different kinds of leaves, twigs, and bark.

Parasites' food requirements are more specialized. Many parasites can survive only in one species of host or in a small group of closely related species. What's more, parasites often live in only one specific part of the host's body, such as the liver, the small intestine, or the skin.

The physical form of parasites is often highly specialized too. During most of its life, the parasitic plant *Rafflesia* is simply a long, threadlike filament living inside the vine that is its host. *Rafflesia* has no leaves, no roots, and no stem. The only time it even looks like a plant is when it flowers and produces a seed-filled fruit.

Some parasites are little more than digestive and reproductive organs. A tapeworm living in a fish's intestine has a head that clamps firmly to the intestinal wall. The rest of the worm is just a long chain of reproductive segments that absorb food from the host and produce millions of eggs.

THE EARLY HISTORY OF PARASITOLOGY

The original meaning of the word *parasite* had nothing to do with biology. In ancient Greece, a parasite was a person who hung around the home of a wealthy patron, waiting for a free meal. In Greek theater, parasites were characters who told amusing stories or did helpful tasks in return for their dinner. The tradition of portraying parasites continued in Roman drama and in Shakespeare's plays. This idea of getting free food from a host is preserved in our modern use of the word *parasite*.

People in earlier times might not have had a special word for parasites, but they certainly knew about some of the terrible problems they cause. Even thousands of years ago, people took precautions to avoid certain parasitic diseases. For example, both the Old Testament of the Bible and the Quran forbid eating pork. This rule may have helped prevent trichinosis, an infection caused by worms that live in hogs.

Early healers certainly knew about parasites. An ancient Egyptian papyrus written about 1500 B.C.E. describes infection of humans by skin parasites and worms. It suggests several treatments.

The Greek philosopher Aristotle (384–322 B.C.E.) wrote about intestinal worms in dogs, pigs, and fish. He also studied the parasitic behavior of the cuckoo, a bird that tricks other songbirds into raising its young. Theophrastus (370–287 B.C.E.), a Greek philosopher, described the parasitic plant *Orobranche*.

The Staff of Asclepius

You may have seen this puzzling symbol at a doctor's office or pharmacy—a serpent wound around a wooden staff. But what do snakes have to do with medical practice? This ancient symbol is called the staff of Asclepius. Asclepius was the Greek god of medicine. The symbol probably comes from a common treatment for parasitic guinea worms.

The larval form of the guinea worm lives inside tiny, shrimplike creatures called copepods. People get infected by drinking water contaminated with copepods. Once inside the human body, the worms grow and mate. The 2-inch-long (5 centimeters) male then dies. The threadlike female worm, which can be up to 3 feet (1 meter) long, finds her way under the skin to her host's leg. The young guinea worms begin to burst out of their mother's reproductive tract. They cause an intense allergic reaction that results in a burning, blistered sore. Eventually the sore breaks open, exposing the female worm. To get relief, the human host is likely to dip his or her leg in water, releasing the young worms. Once in the water, the young worms are eaten by copepods and continue their species' life cycle.

Over a week or two, the female worm gradually works her way out of the sore. If someone tries to pull the worm out all at once, it may break off and cause a potentially deadly infection. To this day, one treatment for guinea worm infection is to gradually wind the worm around a stick as it exits the leg. The staff of Asclepius may simply be a stylized version of this traditional medical procedure.

The Greek physician Hippocrates (ca. 460–ca. 377 B.C.E.) is considered the father of medicine. He knew of worms found in human feces. And the famed Roman physician Galen (129–ca. 199) identified three worms that lived in different regions of the human intestine.

In the tenth century, Arab scholars studied the growth of parasitic plants. They compared these rootless, leafless plants to caterpillars that feed on foliage.

Around 1380 the English writer Chaucer mentioned the parasitic behavior of the cuckoo. Shakespeare too was familiar with this bird's habits. In his play *King Lear*, the court jester warns the king that his daughters may turn against him the way the fledgling cuckoo turns against the sparrow that feeds it.

PARASITOLOGY BECOMES A SCIENCE

There was little scientific study of parasites until the seventeenth century. In 1674 Anton van Leeuwenhoek began peering at tiny living things through the microscopes he built. Van Leeuwenhoek found and described the single-celled parasite *Giardia* living in his own feces. Other scientists used van Leeuwenhoek's microscopes to examine and identify a number of other common parasites.

Scientists of the time also "found" many parasites that existed only in their imaginations. People believed that toothaches were caused by "toothworms." Scientists described and drew worms and other imaginary animals believed to cause diseases ranging from ear infections to the plague.

The Italian scientist Francesco Redi (1626–1697) is considered a founder of modern parasitology. Redi collected and described 108 different species of parasites, including tiny,

Francesco Redi is known as a founder of modern parasitology. In one experiment, Redi set out a covered piece of decaying meat and an uncovered piece. Maggots (fly larvae) appeared on the uncovered meat where flies had laid their eggs. The covered piece of meat had no maggots. Redi's observations led him to dispute the theory of spontaneous generation.

spiderlike mites that cause an itchy skin rash. Redi also published the first book specifically written about parasites.

For about two hundred years, scientists debated a great puzzle: Where do parasites—and other small creatures such as maggots and microbes—come from? How do they suddenly appear in people or for that matter in a bowl of soup left standing for several days? In the 1700s, most scientists believed microbes, maggots, and parasites grew through "spontaneous generation." That is, they simply appeared on their own, as a part of the process of decay. Many naturalists held that belief until the mid-1800s.

Naming Species

Millions of different kinds of creatures populate our world. Each species is a particular kind of organism able to reproduce more of its own kind. A few of the most familiar have common names—crabgrass, earthworms, and mice, for example. But common names can be confusing. Each of the names above is used for a number of different species. On the other hand, most organisms have no common name at all.

To avoid confusion, biologists use a two-word scientific name for each different species they identify. The names are in Latin or are latinized forms of words from other languages. Scientific names allow us to be clear and exact. Suppose you found a crab. It could be any of dozens of different kinds of ten-legged sea creatures with claws. But if you find *Callinectes sapidus (right)*, you know it's the edible blue crab that lives along the Atlantic and Gulf coasts.

The first word in a scientific name, which is capitalized, is the genus name. A genus is a small group of closely related species. For example, *Callinectes* is the genus made up of New World blue crabs. The second word, written in lowercase letters, is the species name. It identifies one particular kind of creature.

After the first mention, writers sometimes abbreviate the genus to just the first letter. For example, *Callinectes sapidus* can be written as *C. sapidus*. And sometimes scientists refer to multiple species within the same genus by using just the genus name.

This naming system was created in the mid-1700s by the Dutch biologist Carolus Linnaeus. Biologists have used it ever since. To identify an organism precisely, scientific names are the best choice, even though they may be difficult to pronounce.

But some scientists disagreed. Organisms can't simply create themselves, they said. New life can only come from the spores or eggs of other living creatures. Perhaps parasites' eggs were inhaled or eaten. Other scientists suggested hosts might be born with parasites already inside them.

In the 1860s, Louis Pasteur finally settled the question. The great French biologist placed meat and other foods in flasks sealed from the outside air. No microbes or maggots grew on the food until he opened the flasks, allowing insects and spores to reach what had been sealed inside. Pasteur had proved that life cannot just appear out of nowhere. Creatures must grow from eggs, spores, or some other source. The hunt was on to find the parasites that plagued humans and to puzzle out their complicated life histories.

Most parasites pass through several different stages in their lives. The process of changing from one form to another is known as metamorphosis. These forms can be so different from one another that early researchers often mistook them for completely different species.

In 1845 J. J. S. Steensrup, a Danish researcher, saw through the confusion. He discovered that certain tiny animals swimming in ponds, cysts (thick-walled capsules enclosing an animal's resting stage) found in snails, and parasitic worms found in the livers of birds were all the same creature. They were all different stages of a species of liver fluke.

In the modern era, science has made great strides in understanding human and agricultural parasites. In the early 1880s, Algernon Thomas and Rudolph Leuckart worked out the complete life cycle of a species of liver fluke that alternates between two different hosts, snails and sheep. In 1881 the Scottish physician Patrick Manson discovered that the worms that cause elephantiasis, a widespread tropical disease, are transmitted by mosquitoes. This was the first evidence that parasites can be spread by insects. In 1897 Ronald Ross discovered that mosquitoes also transmit the parasite that causes malaria. That discovery won him the Nobel Prize in 1902.

By the beginning of the twentieth century, biologists realized how complex parasite life cycles can be. Since then, knowledge about the lives of parasites has exploded. Scientists now know how important parasites are in the web of life. Parasitology is a recognized branch of biology. Nevertheless, parasitology is still a young science. There are surely thousands of parasitic species we don't even know about yet. And there is still much to learn about how parasites affect the lives of other creatures in the natural world.

Chapter Two

PARASITIC FUNGI

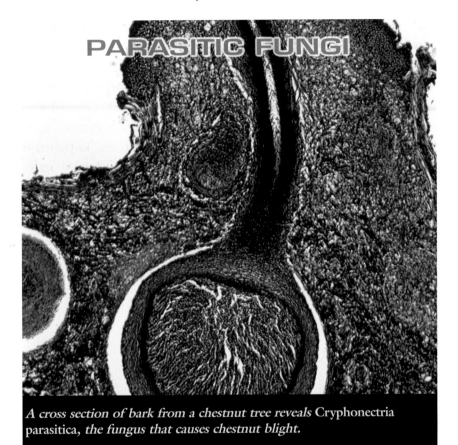

A cross section of bark from a chestnut tree reveals Cryphonectria parasitica, *the fungus that causes chestnut blight.*

Fungi are one of the kingdoms of living creatures, along with the animal and plant kingdoms. Most fungi are decomposers. They live by dissolving and absorbing nutrients from dead plants and animals. They thrive on rotting leaves, fallen trees, and dead animal carcasses. But some fungi don't wait for their food source to die. They get their nutrients from living plants and animals. As they grow, these parasitic fungi can do serious damage to their hosts.

TREE KILLERS

Imagine yourself walking in the woodlands of the eastern United States around 1900. Almost anywhere you look, from New England to Georgia, towering chestnut trees rule the forest. Almost one-quarter of all the deciduous trees (those that lose their leaves each fall) are chestnuts. Carpenters prize their rot-resistant timber for its strength and straight grain. Every autumn the trees provide nutritious nuts for wildlife and for people and their livestock.

Now leap forward to the twenty-first century. Other than a few saplings struggling up from old stumps, there's not a chestnut tree in sight. More than three *billion* chestnut trees are gone from America's forests. The culprit? A parasitic fungus, *Cryphonectria parasitica*, commonly known as chestnut blight.

Chestnut blight was first found in the United States in 1904 at the Bronx Zoo in New York City. It probably came to this country in chestnut trees imported from Japan or China. The fungus also infects Asian chestnuts but rarely kills them.

Foresters tried to stop the disease. They pruned away damaged limbs and cut down infected trees. They even destroyed great swaths of chestnuts to prevent the disease from spreading. Nothing worked. By 1930 the fungus had traveled throughout most of the American chestnut's range. By 1950 almost all adult chestnut trees were gone. Foresters kept the valuable species alive only by growing disease-free shoots in carefully protected groves.

Chestnut blight attacks only the aboveground part of a tree. The old roots often continue to send up new shoots for years. The young saplings grow for ten years or more. But eventually they become infected and die.

The infection begins when a *C. parasitica* spore enters a crack or other wound in a tree's bark. It begins to grow

A chestnut sapling grows from the roots of a tree killed by chestnut blight. The fungus will attack and kill the sapling as well.

beneath the bark. Eventually it forms a canker—a "sore" at the site of the infection. The canker gradually expands around the branch or trunk. It kills the living wood beneath the bark, stopping the flow of water and nutrients. The part of the tree above the canker soon dies.

The fungus produces sticky, yellow-orange spore-producing bodies about the size of a pinhead. These cling to insects or birds, which spread the fungus in their travels. *C. parasitica*'s tiny spores are also carried by the wind to infect distant trees.

Because the chestnut is such a valuable tree, foresters have tried hard to save it. They have used two different strategies to combat the blight and restore at least some chestnuts to American woodlands.

One plan involves breeding blight-resistant trees. Scientists are crossbreeding Asian chestnuts with American chestnut trees. Some of the resulting offspring may be blight-resistant. But it takes years for a tree to grow, flower, and produce seeds. So breeding a resistant strain will take a long time.

The second strategy involves using the parasite against itself. In Italy scientists found a variety of the fungus that is less virulent (harmful). American chestnuts infected by this strain of blight survive. What's more, the less virulent fungus drives out the deadly variety. As the Italian fungus spreads through a grove of trees, the cankers heal and the chestnuts stop dying. Unfortunately, the less virulent variety is not spread by the wind. Nevertheless, it can be used as a biological control in groves where chestnuts grow close together.

Another tree that was common in the eastern United States in the early 1900s is the American elm. Elms were often planted along city streets. They grow quickly and have a tall, graceful shape. Their canopy of leaves creates deep, cooling shade.

Sometime in the 1920s, a shipment of logs from Europe arrived in the United States. The logs included some unwanted guests—European bark beetles. The beetles carried *Ophiostoma ulmi*, the fungus that causes Dutch elm disease.

European elm bark beetles spread the spores of Ophiostoma ulmi, *the fungus that causes Dutch elm disease. Thousands of elm trees in the United States are destroyed every year in an effort to stop the spread of the disease.*

Despite its common name, this parasite is not Dutch. The fungus probably came from Asia, but it was first identified in the Netherlands. The first case of the disease in the United States was discovered in 1930 in Cleveland, Ohio. Since then Dutch elm disease has spread throughout the country, killing more than half of all elm trees.

The fungus causes elms to produce a gummy substance beneath their bark. This substance blocks the flow of water. The fungus spreads under the tree's bark and into the roots. The leaves turn yellow, wilt, and die. Without treatment, the tree dies within a year or two.

O. ulmi produces spores only beneath the bark of infected trees. The spores can't be carried by the wind. So the parasite relies on an insect vector to spread it from tree to tree. Bark beetles bore into the bark of dead or dying trees to lay their eggs. The beetle larvae tunnel under the bark to feed. Adult beetles emerge the following spring with *O. ulmi* spores sticking to their bodies. They fly to other trees, carrying the fungus with them.

O. ulmi can spread in one other way. When elms grow near one another, their roots grow together. The trees develop a shared root system. This often happens on city streets, where elms are planted in long, straight rows. Fungus from one tree travels through the roots to infect other trees nearby.

Foresters have not been able to breed American elms that can resist *O. ulmi*. But if the infection is caught early, they can prolong a tree's life by pruning away the infection and treating the tree with fungicides (chemicals that kill fungi). Close plantings of elms are harder to protect. Infected roots must be cut away from any nearby healthy trees—an expensive, backbreaking task. Dead and dying trees must be cut down and destroyed before the beetles have a chance to spread the infection.

Destroying bark beetles is another way to control the parasite. Insecticides can kill the insects and their larvae.

[THERE'S A FUNGUS AMONG US

Several different species of fungi live on our own skin. They especially like warm, damp places, such as the feet and the groin.

When fungi find a home between our toes, they digest the upper layers of skin. Our skin starts to itch and peel. We have a case of athlete's foot. When fungi grow in the groin area, we call the infection jock itch. Sometimes a fungus may grow on an arm, a cheek, or the scalp. These infections usually create a round, discolored patch we call ringworm. Ringworm looks as if a small, round worm is living just under the skin. But it's not a worm at all. It is a parasitic fungus.

At least four different fungi infect human skin. Doctors call these fungal infections tinea. Tinea pedis (*pedis* is Latin for "foot") is the name for athlete's foot. Ringworm is tinea corporis (*corporis* means "body") or tinea capitis (scalp ringworm). And jock itch is tinea cruris, which comes from the Latin word for "leg." The names refer only to the location of the infection. They do not tell which specific parasite has found a human host. Wherever they grow, fungi cause redness, itching, and peeling skin. They make our skin and nails turn hard and crusty.

Fungus spores can be transmitted directly from person to person by touch. They can also be transmitted by damp surfaces such as locker-room floors. Cats and dogs often carry fungus on their skin and pass it on to their owners.

Athlete's foot is easy to treat. Keep your feet clean and dry and use a medicated cream or powder. Tinea is not usually dangerous to healthy people. Our immune system recognizes invaders such as

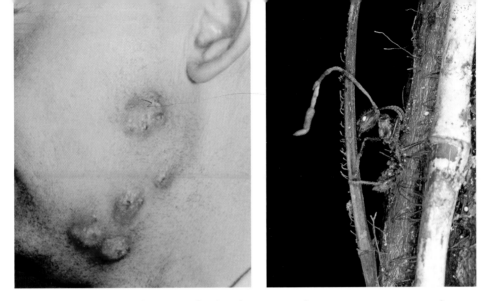

Left: *A parasitic fungus infection known as ringworm appears as red patches on this man's face.* Right: *An ant killed by* Cordyceps fungus. *Note the fungus stalk growing from the ant's body.*

fungi and produces white blood cells and antibodies to attack and destroy them. But severe cases of tinea create cracks in the skin, allowing bacteria to enter and cause infection. Tinea is more serious for people with weakened immune systems, such as people with cancer who are receiving chemotherapy and people with AIDS.

Several other fungi parasitize humans internally. They enter the body through the lungs or an open wound. The best known of these infections is histoplasmosis, a lung ailment. The fungus that causes it is usually found in bird droppings. If left untreated, internal fungus infections can cause severe damage or even death. Fortunately, such infections are rare.

Other animals serve as hosts for fungi too. Insects are parasitized by a variety of fungi. One fungus—a species of *Cordyceps*—brings ants to a gruesome end. When an ant is infected, the fungus gradually spreads through its body. Eventually the ant dies. The fungus sends up a long stalk from the ant's body, with a spore-producing organ at the top. The spores then drift down to infect other ants.

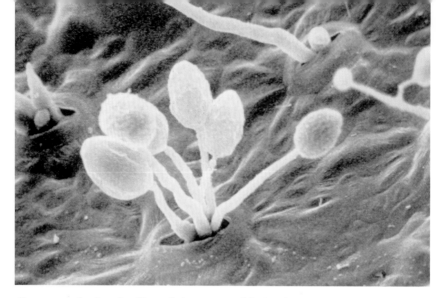

Spore-producing bodies of the potato blight fungus Phytophthora infestans *emerge from the tiny holes of a potato leaf. The fungus caused a deadly potato blight that led to widespread starvation in Ireland in the mid-1800s.*

THE IRISH POTATO FAMINE

How could a fungus that attacks plants cause over one million human deaths?

In the 1800s, most of Ireland's 8.5 million people depended on potatoes for much of their diet. But in 1845, a terrible disease began ruining the Irish potato crop. Known as potato late blight, it is caused by *Phytophthora infestans.* (There is disagreement about what sort of organism *P. infestans* actually is. Some scientists think it is more like algae—simple, single-celled plants—than fungi.)

Potato blight spends the winter in potato tubers—the part of the plant we eat. Farmers plant the tubers in the soil each spring to grow a new crop. If a tuber is infected, the fungus spreads through the stems and leaves as the plant grows. The fungus releases its spores through tiny holes in the plant's leaves. The spores travel on the wind, infecting other plants.

P. infestans spores need rain or dew to germinate, or sprout. The cool, damp Irish climate is perfect for them. The spores actually swim through the moisture on a leaf or in the soil to infect a new plant. The new fungus feeds on the living cells of its host. Later, it gets nutrients from parts of the plant it has killed. Infected potatoes can look perfectly normal when harvested, but they soon turn to a black, inedible mush.

In 1845 Ireland lost more than one-fourth of its potato crop to blight. The following year, almost the entire crop was wiped out. The blight destroyed the potato crop again in 1848. Meanwhile, Ireland's farms were producing plenty of grain and other export crops. But farmworkers and their families were starving. They could not afford to buy the food Ireland grew for export. Unable to pay their rent, many farmers were thrown off the land by wealthy British landlords.

The British government did little to help. More than one million people died of starvation and disease. Another million or more emigrated to the United States and other countries. By 1850 the worst of the famine was over. Farmers planted different varieties of potatoes and more grain. Better relief measures also helped get food to the needy.

Potato blight remains a serious agricultural pest. When weather conditions are favorable for the fungus, farmers must treat their fields with fungicides to kill it. Unfortunately, *P. infestans* has evolved fungicide-resistant strains. Scientists are seeking new chemicals to control the blight, and they are working to breed blight-resistant varieties of potato. The never-ending battle between parasites and hosts continues, even in the simple potato.

Chapter Three

PARASITIC PLANTS

Clumps of mistletoe hang from the branches of an ironwood tree.

We usually think of plants as producers. They use carbon dioxide, water, and sunlight to make food through photosynthesis. But at least three thousand plant species live as parasites, stealing nutrients from other plants. Some parasitic plants are small and easy to overlook. Others grow to the size of full-grown trees. The most familiar parasitic plants are those that damage food crops or trees that people use for lumber. But unless you are a farmer or a forester, you may not know about these unusual organisms.

Most parasitic plants tap into the system of cells that transports water and nutrients from the roots to the leaves. Some parasites get nutrients directly from the roots of their host. Botanists refer to them as root parasites. Others, called stem parasites, steal food and water from a plant's stems, branches, or trunk.

About 20 percent of parasitic plant species, such as mistletoe, can make some of their own food through photosynthesis. The rest have little or no chlorophyll, the chemical that allows plants to turn water and carbon dioxide into sugars. They rely entirely on their hosts for nutrients.

MISTLETOE

High in the branches of a fir tree, a small bird wipes its beak to remove some sticky mistletoe seeds. Soon one of those seeds sprouts, sending a root tip down into the bark of the tree. Over the next several months, the growing plant sends out rootlike haustoria that spread through the wood and tap into the tree's own supply of sap. Nutrients and water intended for the tree itself now feed the growing clump of mistletoe instead.

Mistletoe is probably the best-known plant parasite. Hundreds of different species of mistletoe live on all the world's continents except Antarctica. It grows almost everywhere in North America. Mistletoe is an evergreen—it keeps its leaves all year long. It is easy to spot because it often lives in the branches of deciduous trees, which lose their leaves each fall. In the winter, clumps of dark green mistletoe leaves can be seen high among the bare branches. Some mistletoes parasitize only one particular kind of tree, while others can infect many different species.

Let's take a look at the life cycle of dwarf mistletoe (*Arceuthobium* species), a parasite of evergreen trees such as pines. Dwarf mistletoe fruits are explosive when ripe. At the slightest touch, they fire their sticky seeds into the air. The seeds can fly more

Dwarf mistletoe grows on the branches of a Jeffrey pine. To curb the spread of dwarf mistletoe, forestry workers must cut away infected tree limbs.

than 50 feet (15 m). If a seed sticks to the branch of a tree, it absorbs water from rain or dew and germinates. Its root tip penetrates the branch at the base of a needle. The external part of the seed then dies, while the parasite grows inside the tree branch.

The mistletoe plant develops a network of haustoria within the wood of its host. The tree's sap supplies water and nutrients. After many months, the parasite sends shoots out through the tree's bark. Then it flowers. Mistletoe plants are either male or female. The flowers of a female plant must be fertilized by pollen from a male plant to produce a new crop of seeds.

Trees usually survive an infestation of mistletoe, but infected trees may become stunted or deformed. Mistletoe can even kill weaker young trees. To combat mistletoe, a forester must prune away the infected branches. Dwarf mistletoe is particularly hard to control because the parasite stays hidden for a year or more before its leaves become visible.

DODDER

You may have seen dodder growing among other plants and wondered just what you were looking at. It looks more like a tangle of orange or yellow fishing line than a plant. Dodder has no visible leaves. The long, threadlike plant wraps around the stems and leaves of other plants. Because of its unusual appearance and growth habits, its common names include strangleweed, devil's hair, hellbind, gold thread, and love vine.

More than one hundred species of dodder grow throughout the world. Dodder starts life as a small seed on the ground. The seed germinates and puts out a temporary root. Then a long stem grows upward until it touches a host plant. The stem winds itself around the host, then develops haustoria. The haustoria enter the

Yellow, stringlike dodder (Cuscuta) encases plants from which it gets water and nutrients.

host and begin stealing water and nutrients. The dodder's own roots then die away. Mature dodder plants are completely disconnected from the ground. Dodder has little or no chlorophyll to produce its own food. It is entirely dependent on its host.

As it grows, a single dodder plant reaches out to entangle other nearby plants. Eventually it can produce a snarl of stems that would be hundreds of yards long if they were stretched end to end. The host plants become weak and discolored from strangulation and loss of nutrients.

In late summer or fall, dodder produces clusters of small yellow or white flowers that produce many small, tough seeds. These seeds stay viable (able to germinate) for up to five years. Dodder can also regrow from small pieces of stem broken or cut from the original plant.

Dodder looks thin and weak. But this parasite does a lot of damage. It is especially harmful to farm crops such as clover, alfalfa, and flax. Once dodder has taken hold in a field, it's hard to destroy. Farmers can control dodder by planting clean seed and by mowing down infested sections of their fields. Dodder can also be controlled with herbicides (chemicals used to kill unwanted plants).

WITCHWEED AND BROOMRAPE

Striga, or witchweed, is probably the most destructive plant you've never heard of. About a dozen different parasitic species of *Striga* grow throughout Africa and in much of Asia. In Africa they cause more crop loss than insects, birds, or disease. Witchweed sinks its haustoria into the roots of crops such as corn, millet, sorghum, rice, and cowpeas. *Striga* attacks many species of wild plants as well. Since *Striga* has no chlorophyll of its own, it is completely dependent on its host for nutrients.

Witchweed sprouts at the base of a corn plant.

Tiny *Striga* seeds germinate only when stimulated by chemicals from the roots of a potential host. The witchweed root follows those chemical signals to the host root and begins developing its haustoria. If it cannot find a host within four days of germinating, the seed runs out of stored food and dies.

Once witchweed finds a host, it sends out more haustoria to make contact with other host roots. For five or six weeks, the parasite grows hidden underground. *Striga* weakens its host long before it sprouts at the base of the plant. The damage to the host plant from the invisible parasite seems supernatural. This is the source of the common name witchweed. About two weeks after it emerges, *Striga* begins to flower. A month later, the plant sheds its seeds, completing its life cycle.

Witchweed's seeds are one of the main reasons for its success. A single plant produces up to two hundred thousand seeds. They are as tiny as specks of dust. It takes as many as eight million seeds to weigh 1 ounce (30 grams). It's not surprising that *Striga* spreads through a farmer's field so effectively.

Striga takes both nutrients and water from its host. A plant parasitized by witchweed grows stunted and weak. Infected plants have more difficulty surviving periods of drought. A severe witchweed infection can kill a plant before it reaches maturity.

Another group of root parasites, called *Orobranche,* or broomrape, has a similar life cycle. Like witchweed, broomrape has no chlorophyll. It too produces huge numbers of dustlike seeds that can remain dormant for years before sprouting. Broomrapes are major agricultural pests in the Mediterranean region and in other parts of Europe and Asia. Some broomrapes grow in the southern and western United States, where they parasitize a wide variety of species, including a number of crops.

STRANGLER FIG

The strangler fig is an amazing rain forest tree. In Spanish it is called *matapalo,* or "tree killer." It doesn't take nutrients or water from its host. Instead, it steals sunlight.

In the rain forest, sunlight is precious. Towering trees spread their branches high above the forest floor, forming a dense canopy. Very little sun reaches the ground. Seedlings must struggle to reach the light quickly. Unless there's a clearing in the canopy, most die from lack of sun.

The strangler fig has a unique strategy to win this life-or-death competition. It produces sweet fruits prized by birds, monkeys, and other animals. High in a tree, fig seeds from an

Strangler fig roots completely encase this host tree.

animal's droppings sprout on a moist, mossy branch. The young seedlings send out long, vinelike roots toward the ground far below. Once the vines reach the ground, the plants send out more roots to gather water and nutrients. The figs quickly grow stronger.

Most strangler figs are made up of several individual plants that have grown together. The roots branch out and merge, enclosing the trunk of the host tree in a sturdy wooden web. The fig doesn't actually "strangle" its host. The vines simply prevent it from growing any larger. Meanwhile, the fig spreads its branches and steals the sunlight once used by its host. Eventually the host tree dies. The fig remains standing, a huge tree with a hollow trunk.

About three hundred species of strangler figs grow in tropical and semitropical regions of the world, including Florida. Some grow to heights of about 150 feet (45 m). They are among the most important plants in the rain forest. They produce fruit year-round, so many creatures depend on them for food. The hollow trunk makes a good home for forest creatures, from small insects to large mammals.

RAFFLESIA

The world's largest and stinkiest flower is produced by a parasitic plant. *Rafflesia arnoldii* and several other related species live in the islands of Indonesia. These plants have no roots, leaves, stems, or chlorophyll. *Rafflesia* spends most of its life as a threadlike growth inside its host, a vine in the grape family. It's not clear how damaging this parasite is to its host.

When it is ready to flower, *Rafflesia* produces a cabbagelike bud. The bud takes about a year to develop. Eventually it opens into a huge orange and brown blossom about 3 feet (1 m) across. The flower can weigh more than 20 pounds (about 10 kilograms).

The bloom smells like rotting meat. The odor attracts flies and beetles to pollinate the flower. After a few days, the flower decomposes into a slimy black mass. The plant produces a fruit full of tiny seeds that are probably spread by small mammals.

Rafflesia is quite rare and grows in only a limited area. Thousands of tourists visit Indonesia each year, hoping to see

*A foul-smelling **Rafflesia** flower blooms in a rain forest in Indonesia. This exotic plant has no roots, leaves, or stems of its own. It depends on its host plant for all of its nutrients.*

these bizarre flowers in bloom. Scientists have recently learned how to grow the plant in a laboratory setting. They hope this new knowledge will help them preserve this threatened species.

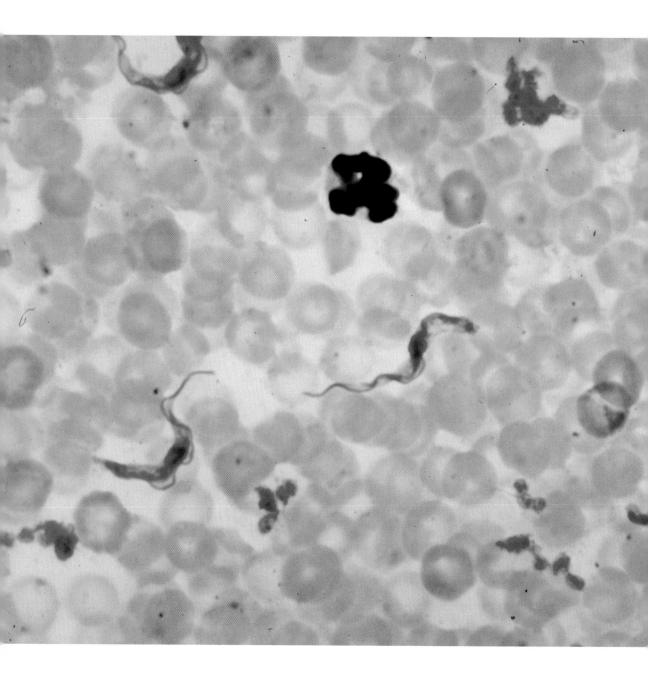

Chapter Four

SINGLE-CELLED PARASITES

Many Africans don't have enough to eat. Meanwhile, the center of the continent has vast stretches of fertile grassland. The land seems ideal for raising cattle or other farm animals. But no farmers or ranchers live there. An area measuring 4.5 million square miles (nearly 12 million square kilometers)—larger than the entire United States—cannot be used for grazing. Why not?

The answer is a creature so small it can be seen only with a microscope. It is a protozoan (single-celled animal) called *Trypanosoma brucei.*

T. brucei lives in the blood of vertebrates (animals with backbones). The parasite is transmitted through the bite of a tsetse fly. It causes a disease called nagana that kills sheep, goats, cattle, horses, and other farm animals. Raising livestock is almost impossible in the wide band of central Africa where tsetse flies live. Wild grazing animals like antelope serve as a source of infection. Tsetse flies bite the native animals, then transfer the parasite to domestic species.

Protozoa cause more human death and disease than any other parasites. Trypanosomes similar to those that cause nagana are responsible for sleeping sickness and Chagas disease in people. Malaria too is caused by a protozoan. *Leishmania*, transmitted by

A blood smear from a rat contains Trypanosoma brucei *(in dark purple), the single-celled parasite that causes the diseases sleeping sickness and nagana.*

Intermediate hosts, such as tsetse flies (above) *and mosquitoes, spread blood-borne parasites by drawing blood from an infected host and then biting other hosts.*

biting sandflies, infects millions of people. Amoebas cause potentially fatal intestinal illness. Let's find out how some of these tiny organisms live, reproduce, and travel from host to host.

MALARIA

In a Nigerian village, a four-year-old child lies huddled under a blanket. He is racked with fever and chills. His mother sits beside him. She gives him sips of water from a bowl and tries to comfort him. She has given him the medicine she got from the village clinic. Now she can only cool her son's fever with a damp cloth and wait to see if he is strong enough to fight off the parasites flooding his bloodstream.

Malaria kills more people each year than any other disease except tuberculosis and dysentery. It has defeated armies and changed the course of history. Scientists estimate there are as many as five hundred million cases a year. Each year about 2.5 million people die from the disease, many of them young children. The disease causes billions of dollars in economic losses.

Malaria means "bad air." For centuries people thought the disease was caused by breathing the humid air of swamps and marshland. Its true cause was a mystery until 1880, when Louis Alveran, a French army physician, found *Plasmodium* in the blood of malaria patients. In 1897 British army physician Ronald Ross discovered that *Plasmodium* is transmitted through mosquito bites. For these parasites, human beings are intermediate hosts. Mosquitoes are their definitive hosts. Four different species of *Plasmodium* cause malaria in humans. Other *Plasmodium* species cause malaria in mammals and birds.

Thanks to Ross's discovery, some control of the disease became possible. For example, for years malaria and yellow fever (another disease transmitted by mosquitoes) prevented construction of the Panama Canal in Central America. Then William Gorgas, the medical officer in charge of the Canal Zone, started a program of mosquito control. Workers sprayed insecticide, eliminated mosquito breeding sites, and installed window screens and mosquito netting. These efforts cut malaria by more than 90 percent. The program saved thousands of lives and made building the canal possible. In the twenty-first century, mosquito control is still the most effective way to fight malaria.

The Life Cycle of *Plasmodium*

A protozoan is a single cell. But that doesn't mean its life is simple. *Plasmodium* passes through several different stages within its hosts.

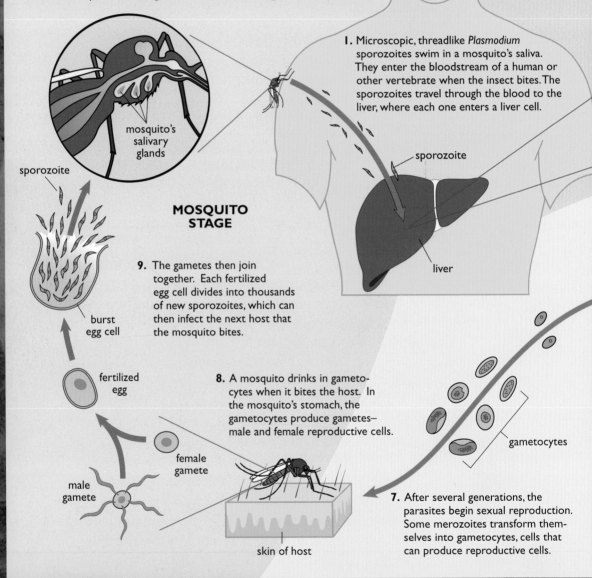

mosquito's salivary glands

1. Microscopic, threadlike *Plasmodium* sporozoites swim in a mosquito's saliva. They enter the bloodstream of a human or other vertebrate when the insect bites. The sporozoites travel through the blood to the liver, where each one enters a liver cell.

sporozoite

liver

sporozoite

MOSQUITO STAGE

9. The gametes then join together. Each fertilized egg cell divides into thousands of new sporozoites, which can then infect the next host that the mosquito bites.

burst egg cell

fertilized egg

8. A mosquito drinks in gametocytes when it bites the host. In the mosquito's stomach, the gametocytes produce gametes—male and female reproductive cells.

gametocytes

female gamete

male gamete

skin of host

7. After several generations, the parasites begin sexual reproduction. Some merozoites transform themselves into gametocytes, cells that can produce reproductive cells.

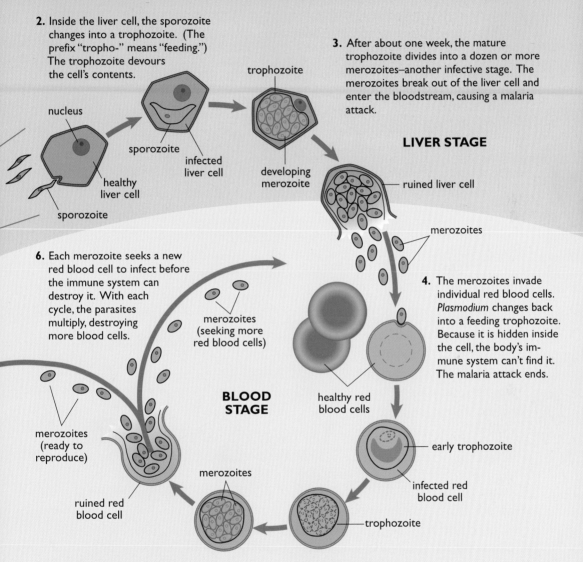

2. Inside the liver cell, the sporozoite changes into a trophozoite. (The prefix "tropho-" means "feeding.") The trophozoite devours the cell's contents.

3. After about one week, the mature trophozoite divides into a dozen or more merozoites–another infective stage. The merozoites break out of the liver cell and enter the bloodstream, causing a malaria attack.

nucleus

sporozoite

infected liver cell

trophozoite

developing merozoite

healthy liver cell

sporozoite

LIVER STAGE

ruined liver cell

merozoites

6. Each merozoite seeks a new red blood cell to infect before the immune system can destroy it. With each cycle, the parasites multiply, destroying more blood cells.

merozoites (seeking more red blood cells)

4. The merozoites invade individual red blood cells. *Plasmodium* changes back into a feeding trophozoite. Because it is hidden inside the cell, the body's immune system can't find it. The malaria attack ends.

BLOOD STAGE

healthy red blood cells

merozoites (ready to reproduce)

early trophozoite

infected red blood cell

merozoites

ruined red blood cell

trophozoite

5. After one to four days–depending on the species–the trophozoite again divides to form merozoites. The ruined red blood cell bursts open, spilling the merozoites and their wastes into the bloodstream. Perhaps because merozoites mature at a similar rate, they all break out of the blood cells at about the same time. The synchronized timing gives malaria its characteristic symptoms–bouts of chills and fever alternating with periods when the victim feels better.

Plasmodium parasites multiply in the liver for about one week before entering the bloodstream and causing the first symptoms to appear. An attack of malaria comes on suddenly. The victim suffers high fever and chills, along with nausea and severe headaches. The symptoms are caused by the victim's own immune system as it attacks the parasites and their waste products in the blood.

After about half a day, the parasites have entered red blood cells. The victim's fever breaks, and he or she sweats heavily. The person usually feels better until a flood of parasites breaks out of blood cells several days later. The parasites enter intact red blood cells, and the cycle repeats. The destruction of red blood cells leaves the victim anemic and weak.

Each of the four different species of *Plasmodium* that affect humans causes slightly different symptoms. *Plasmodium falciparum* is by far the most dangerous, especially to young children. People who survive their first infection develop some resistance to future attacks. Later infections, while serious, are less deadly.

Malaria was once common in much of Europe and North America, including the United States. Thanks to mosquito control and antimalarial drugs, the disease is now very rare outside the tropics. There are only about one thousand cases of malaria each year in the United States, mostly among people who have traveled to tropical countries. But malaria is still a plague in humid tropical and subtropical areas of the world.

In the 1600s, European explorers learned from native South American healers that the bark of the cinchona tree could be made into a bitter tea that combats the parasite. Quinine, a drug extracted from cinchona bark, has been used to treat malaria ever since. During World War II (1939–1945), when supplies of cinchona from Pacific plantations were cut off, scientists created synthetic drugs similar to quinine. Unfortunately, some strains of *Plasmodium* have evolved resistance to these drugs. In the 1980s, additional drugs were developed from qing-hao, an herb also known as sweet wormwood or artemisia. This antimalarial herb has been used in traditonal Chinese medicine for two thousand years.

Scientists are developing a vaccine to immunize people against *Plasmodium*. Such a vaccine could save millions of lives around the world.

FLAGELLATES

Trypanosomes are flagellates, single-celled creatures that propel themselves with a whiplike flagellum. The name *trypanosome* comes from the Greek word for "auger," a tool used for boring holes. These parasites are shaped like flattened spirals. When they swim, their bodies spin like a drill.

There are many species of parasitic trypanosomes, including several that infect humans and domestic animals. The three varieties of *Trypanosoma brucei* cause the greatest problems for people. They are responsible for the African diseases nagana and sleeping sickness.

Several thousand trypanosomes enter the blood with the bite of a single infected tsetse fly. Like *Plasmodium*, these parasites go through several different stages during their life cycle.

Trypanosomes don't live inside cells as *Plasmodium* does. They live in the blood and lymph—the clear body fluid that contains only white blood cells. They especially favor the fluid surrounding the spinal cord and brain.

Vertebrates, including humans, have very effective immune systems. Our blood produces antibodies to defend against

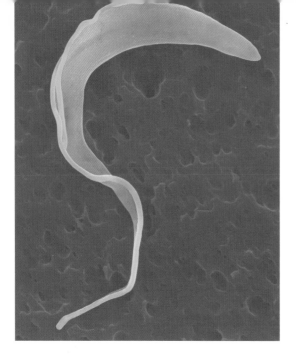

Trypanosomes propel themselves with their whiplike tails.

foreign proteins, such as those that form the outer coating of a trypanosome. But trypanosomes have evolved a way to out-smart the immune system. When the invading parasites are attacked, some of them change the proteins that coat their bodies. The immune system has no antibodies to fight the new proteins, so the trypanosomes can multiply undisturbed. When the immune system starts to produce antibodies to attack the new version of the parasite, it changes its proteins again. Scientists have seen trypanosomes make this change over one hundred times during the course of an infection. The body's immune system never catches up.

About twenty million Africans are infected with *Trypanosoma brucei*. If untreated, the disease is fatal in a few months. The symptoms include drowsiness, loss of alertness, loss of coordination, and paralysis. These symptoms give the disease its common name, sleeping sickness. A number of drugs can halt the disease if they are given early enough, but the drugs themselves are quite toxic.

Another trypanosome, *Trypanosoma cruzi*, infects almost twenty million people in Central and South America. It causes Chagas disease, named for the biologist who first found the parasite. *T. cruzi* is transmitted by several species of biting insect. It damages the heart and the nerves that serve it. The infection can cause death by heart failure. The great biologist Charles Darwin is believed to have suffered from Chagas disease.

Leishmania are another group of flagellates. Three different species of *Leishmania* infect about eighty million humans, causing a variety of diseases. They are found in tropical regions of Africa, Asia, and Latin America. All enter the bloodstream with the bite of tiny sandflies. *Leishmania*'s method of outwitting the immune system is similar to that used by HIV, the virus that causes AIDS. White blood cells called macrophages are supposed to surround and digest foreign invaders. But *Leishmania* turns the tables on these immune cells. It feeds on the macrophage, then reproduces by division. The parasites break out of the dead cells and go on to feed on more macrophages.

AMOEBAS AND *GIARDIA*

An animal's intestine is warm, protected, and full of food. It's not surprising that many parasites find it an ideal home. They can make our lives pretty miserable in the process.

The amoeba *Entamoeba histolytica* infects more than five hundred million people worldwide. Only about one quarter of them suffer any illness, but anyone who carries the amoebas can pass them on in their wastes. People usually get infected by eating contaminated food or drinking contaminated water. As you might expect, places with poor sanitation have more infections. In the United States, about 5 percent of the population is infected.

E. hystolytica can cause amoebic dysentery. Symptoms include severe intestinal inflammation with stomach pain, bloody diarrhea, and dehydration. Holes may form in the intestine, leading to more widespread infection. Severe cases can be fatal. Fortunately, a number of drugs can treat amoebic infections successfully.

Giardia duodenalis (also known as *Giardia lamblia*) is a flagellate that is common throughout the world, including the United States. It causes an infection called giardiasis. People are ordinarily infected by drinking water contaminated by human waste or that of animals, such as dogs, sheep, and beavers. A cool, clear stream or pond may look inviting, but its water could be teeming with *Giardia*.

Many infected people have no symptoms. But *Giardia* is very contagious—a good reason to wash your hands. Giardiasis is not fatal, but it is unpleasant. The parasite multiplies and coats the lining of the lower intestine, preventing its host from absorbing water and nutrients. The infection causes diarrhea, intestinal gas, dehydration, and pain. Giardiasis can be treated with drugs.

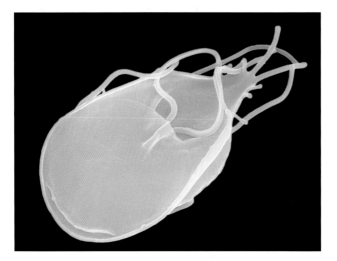

Giardia *may look like a creature from outer space, but it is actually a single-celled parasite that lives in the intestines of mammals and causes unpleasant intestinal symptoms.*

TOXOPLASMA GONDII AND *CRYPTOSPORIDIUM*

Some parasites ordinarily spend their lives in animals. But if they have the chance, they also infect humans. Such an infection is called a zoonosis.

Two protozoa that cause zoonoses have gotten a lot of attention in recent years. One is *Toxoplasma gondii*, the organism that causes toxoplasmosis. *Toxoplasma* is primarily a parasite of cats, although it is common in other vertebrates too. *Toxoplasma* in wastewater dumped into the Pacific Ocean has killed sea otters. People can become infected by eating contaminated raw or undercooked meat, especially pork, lamb, and venison.

Insects, especially flies and cockroaches, pick up *Toxoplasma* from a cat's feces. The parasite then infects intermediate hosts, including birds and rodents. When another cat kills and eats one of these intermediate hosts, it becomes infected.

In the United States, about half of us have *Toxoplasma* living inside us. The parasite rarely produces serious symptoms in humans. But it can be dangerous during pregnancy. Toxoplasmosis occasionally causes disability or death of a developing fetus. People with weakened immune systems may have trouble resisting a *Toxoplasma* infection that would be harmless to others.

Cryptosporidium is another parasite that ordinarily infects domestic animals, including turkeys, chickens, calves, and lambs. The several species of *Cryptosporidium* are intestinal parasites, passed on through an animal's feces. Humans who live or work with animals may become infected. Occasionally *Cryptosporidium* has contaminated a city water supply. For most people, the parasite doesn't cause serious illness. People with weakened immune systems may not be able to fight it off, however. As yet, there is no effective drug treatment for *Cryptosporidium*.

Chapter Five

PARASITIC WORMS

One type of flatworm, Fasciola hepatica *(the liver fluke),* infects the livers of grazing mammals.

A young teacher in Botswana studies her pupils. She's noticed that three of her students seem to have little energy for study or play. She knows that the children may have an infection of parasitic flatworms. The streams where the children swim and where families do their washing are infested with the worms. Children can be infected just by wading in the water. Treatment is available at the clinic, if the doctors and nurses are alerted that someone needs it.

The word *worm* has little scientific meaning. It describes any invertebrate (an animal without a backbone) with a long, thin body. A more formal term for these animals is *helminths*. Biologists recognize several different phyla (major groups) of helminths. They include flatworms (*Platyhelminthes*), roundworms (*Nematoda*), thorny headed worms (*Acanthocephala*), and several other groups. These phyla of animals have little in common except the shape of their bodies.

Often several different kinds of worms live in a single host. For example, a deer might have three species of worms living in its intestines and others inhabiting its liver, lungs, and brain.

Parasitologists have identified 342 different species of worms that parasitize humans. There are more worm infections among people than the total number of human beings in the world. That doesn't mean every single person is infected. Many people host several different species of worm at the same time.

Most parasitic worms require at least two hosts to complete their life cycles. They reproduce within the body of their definitive host. The eggs or larvae leave that host and enter the environment. The larval worms must find an intermediate host. Only then can they make their way to another definitive host, develop into adults, and reproduce.

FLUKES AND SCHISTOSOMES

Flukes are members of the flatworm phylum, *Platyhelminthes*. The liver fluke, *Fasciola hepatica*, is among the best known. It is a major parasite of sheep, cattle, and other grazing animals. Heavy infestations of liver flukes cause a disease called liver rot that can kill these animals. More than two million humans are also infected with this parasite.

The Life Cycle of the Liver Fluke

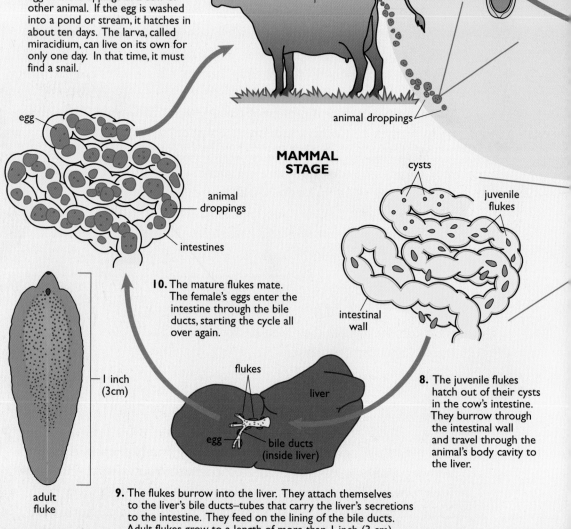

1. *Fasciola hepatica* begins life as an egg in the droppings of a cow or other animal. If the egg is washed into a pond or stream, it hatches in about ten days. The larva, called miracidium, can live on its own for only one day. In that time, it must find a snail.

infected animal

egg containing miracidium

animal droppings

egg

animal droppings

intestines

MAMMAL STAGE

cysts

juvenile flukes

intestinal wall

10. The mature flukes mate. The female's eggs enter the intestine through the bile ducts, starting the cycle all over again.

flukes

liver

I inch (3cm)

egg

bile ducts (inside liver)

adult fluke

8. The juvenile flukes hatch out of their cysts in the cow's intestine. They burrow through the intestinal wall and travel through the animal's body cavity to the liver.

9. The flukes burrow into the liver. They attach themselves to the liver's bile ducts—tubes that carry the liver's secretions to the intestine. They feed on the lining of the bile ducts. Adult flukes grow to a length of more than 1 inch (3 cm).

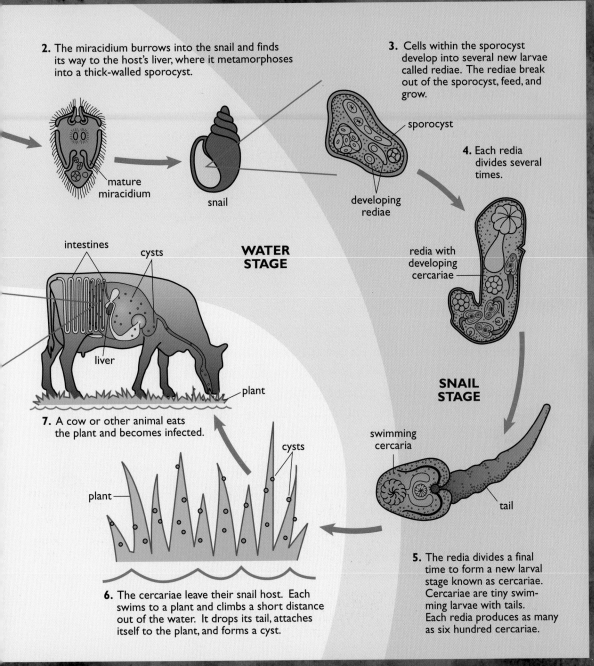

2. The miracidium burrows into the snail and finds its way to the host's liver, where it metamorphoses into a thick-walled sporocyst.

mature miracidium

snail

3. Cells within the sporocyst develop into several new larvae called rediae. The rediae break out of the sporocyst, feed, and grow.

sporocyst

developing rediae

4. Each redia divides several times.

redia with developing cercariae

intestines

cysts

WATER STAGE

liver

plant

SNAIL STAGE

7. A cow or other animal eats the plant and becomes infected.

cysts

swimming cercaria

plant

tail

6. The cercariae leave their snail host. Each swims to a plant and climbs a short distance out of the water. It drops its tail, attaches itself to the plant, and forms a cyst.

5. The redia divides a final time to form a new larval stage known as cercariae. Cercariae are tiny swimming larvae with tails. Each redia produces as many as six hundred cercariae.

Three species of schistosomes, also known as blood flukes, infect about three hundred million people in Africa, Asia, and parts of South America. They have life cycles similar to that of the liver fluke. They cause a disease called schistosomiasis.

Schistosomiasis is most common where local waterways are contaminated with human waste. People become infected when they wade in contaminated ponds, streams, or irrigation ditches. The larvae burrow into their skin and travel to their internal organs. Each species of schistosome causes slightly different symptoms, but all three severely damage the liver and other organs. If left untreated, the infection can eventually be fatal. Fortunately, schistosomiasis can be treated with a variety of drugs.

TAPEWORMS

Tapeworms live in the intestines of vertebrates. They are flatworms, but their lives are very different from those of flukes. Tapeworms get their name from their long, flat shape. An adult tapeworm has a head, called a scolex, with hooks, spines, or suckers that it uses to cling to the intestinal wall. A long chain of flat segments called proglottids grow behind the head, one after another.

Tapeworms have no mouth and no digestive system. They don't need them. A tapeworm lives in an intestine, surrounded by food. It simply absorbs nutrients through its skin. Tapeworms grow quite large and steal much of the nutrition that would otherwise benefit their host.

Tapeworms don't make people ravenously hungry, despite what folklore tells us. A tapeworm infection is more likely to cause loss of appetite, along with diarrhea or constipation, dizziness, abdominal pain, and nausea.

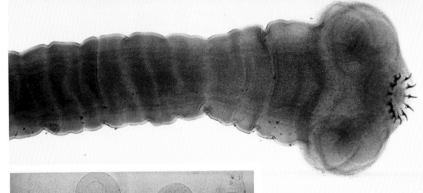

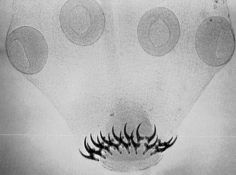

Tapeworms use hooks, spines, or suckers to attach to their hosts' intestinal lining. They absorb half-digested food through their skin.

Each proglottid contains a complete reproductive system. It can fertilize its own eggs, mate with other proglottids from the same worm, or mate with a proglottid from another worm. The proglottid matures as it moves toward the end of the worm. Then it drops off. The tapeworm's eggs pass out of the host's body with its feces. An intermediate host becomes infected when it eats the eggs.

Taenia saginatus, the beef tapeworm, is the species most often found in humans. Almost eighty million people are infected worldwide. Another ten million are infected with *T. solium*, the pork tapeworm. This worm is far more dangerous than *T. saginatus*. That's because humans can also become infected as intermediate hosts.

Adult pork tapeworms live in the small intestine of humans and other carnivores (meat eaters). They ordinarily grow to a length of 6 to 10 feet (about 2 to 3 m), but worms as long as

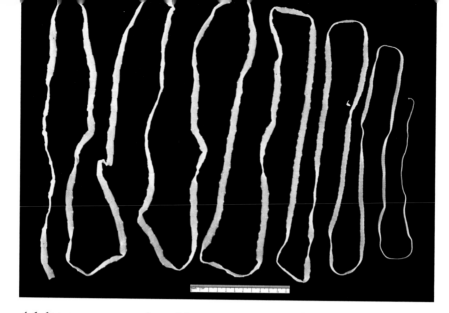

Adult tapeworms, such as this one, can grow to be as long as a three-story building is tall.

30 feet (almost 10 m) have been reported. A pork tapeworm can survive in the intestine for as long as twenty-five years.

As with other tapeworms, the eggs pass out of the intestine with the feces. The usual intermediate host for *T. solium* is a pig. The pig eats some of the eggs, which hatch in its intestine. The worm larvae burrow through the intestinal lining and enter a vein. The blood carries them throughout the pig's body. Eventually the larvae leave the bloodstream, enter the muscles, and form cysts. A person or other carnivore becomes infected by eating undercooked pork. The juvenile worm escapes from its cyst and attaches itself to the host's small intestine. In five to twelve weeks, the worm matures and begins producing eggs.

If a person consumes *T. solium* eggs, the larvae migrate through his or her body and form cysts, just as they would in a pig. The host's body surrounds the cysts with a fibrous growth to isolate them. When an encysted worm dies, the person's immune system attacks it. The resulting inflammation can be fatal, especially if the infection is in the brain.

People can infect themselves or others with tapeworm eggs if they don't wash their hands after using the bathroom. Vegetables grown in gardens fertilized with human waste are another source of infection. Fortunately, the pork tapeworm is rarely found in the United States or Canada.

NEMATODES

Nematodes, or roundworms, are everywhere. The name *nematode* comes from *nema*, the Greek word for "thread." As many as nine billion of these tiny worms live in a single acre (0.4 hectare) of farmland. Biologists claim that if all matter except for nematodes were to magically disappear, the ghostly shapes of our familiar world would still remain. Soil, plants, and animals could still be seen, all made up of the trillions of nematodes that had been left behind.

Some nematode species live freely in the soil, and in freshwater and salt water. Some eat algae or fungi. Others are predators. The phylum Nematoda also includes some of the most destructive parasites of humans.

ROOT NEMATODES

Tiny worms we never see cause terrible damage to crops around the world. Many different kinds of nematodes infect the roots of plants. The U.S. Department of Agriculture estimates that root nematodes cause eighty billion dollars in crop losses each year worldwide. Every crop has at least one species of nematode parasite. Some have many more. Soybeans, for example, are attacked by more than fifty different kinds of nematodes.

Root nematodes are small enough to swim through the moisture in the soil. Full-grown adults are usually no longer than 0.1 inch (3 millimeters). They are transparent and difficult to see. Their eggs and larvae are microscopic.

To feed, a root nematode pierces the root of a plant with the sharp, needlelike mouth. The worm injects chemicals that damage the plant's cells, then feeds on their contents. Some root nematodes move from place to place on the outside of the root as they feed. Others bore inside the root. Still other nematodes enter the plant and damage stems and leaves. Plant roots grow knots or twists in response to these attacks.

Nematodes rob a plant of nutrients and water and stunt its growth. They also can transmit disease-causing viruses and bacteria. Infested plants produce smaller crops and are less resistant to drought and disease.

After nematodes mate, the female produces from fifty to several thousand eggs, depending on the species. In warm, moist soil, a root nematode grows from an egg to a mature adult in just three to four weeks.

Nematode populations peak in late summer. Eggs laid at the end of the growing season remain in the soil during the winter. Farmers can use pesticides to kill the worms. Rotating crops—growing different crops in a field from year to year—also helps to prevent a nematode population explosion.

TRICHINELLA

One of the most dangerous of all human parasites is the nematode *Trichinella spiralis. Trichinella* can live in most mammals.

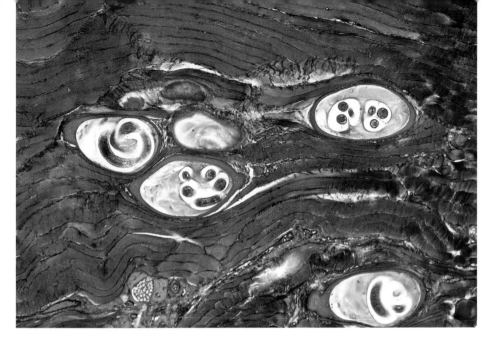

A cross section of muscle tissue reveals cysts formed by young Trichinella *roundworms. People who eat undercooked meat risk becoming infected by* Trichinella.

Hosts become infected by eating the flesh of other animals. So *Trichinella* is most common in carnivores such as bears, rodents, cats, dogs, and even walruses.

The adult stage of *Trichinella* is short-lived. Adult females are about 0.1 inch (3 mm) long. Males are half that size. Adult males and females live and mate in the intestine. Males die after mating, but the females live from one to four months. During this time, they give birth to about fifteen hundred juvenile worms.

Trichinella's life cyle is unusual in that the same animal can serve as both definitive host and intermediate host. Some juvenile worms pass out of the definitive host with its feces and can infect other animals. But many of the juveniles remain in the original host.

Trichinosis (*Trichinella* infection) has some similarities to infection by the pork tapeworm. The juvenile worms travel in the bloodstream and find their way to a muscle. Each tiny worm penetrates a muscle cell. It coils inside the muscle (hence the name *spiralis*) and forms a cyst. The worm can survive in its cyst for many months. An animal that eats the infected meat becomes infected.

People in northern latitudes who rely on hunting for food can contract trichinosis by eating raw or undercooked game, especially bear or walrus. For the rest of us, the most common source of infection is undercooked pork. Just 1 ounce (about 28 g) of infected meat can contain more than one hundred thousand juvenile worms. Even a bite or two of heavily infected pork can be fatal.

Fortunately, trichinosis is completely preventable. Heat kills any encysted worms. That is why it's so important to cook pork until it is no longer pink. Freezing at 5°F (−15°C) for twenty days or more also kills the worms.

HOOKWORMS

Hookworms live their adult lives in the intestines of humans and many other animals. These nematodes have wide mouths with sharp teeth or other grasping organs. They grab the intestinal wall and feed on blood and other body fluids.

Hookworms thrive in tropical and semitropical regions. Around the world, about one billion people are infected. Hookworms are a problem in places where people often walk barefoot and the ground is contaminated with human waste.

Hookworms depend on a single host. Hookworm eggs pass out of their host in feces. The eggs need warmth, shade, and moisture to develop. In about two days, they hatch into larval worms. The larvae live in the soil and feed on plant matter and feces. After about a week, they metamorphose into their infective stage. When the ground is damp, the tiny worms wait at the soil's surface, seeking an exposed patch of skin, such as a bare foot or leg. When a worm contacts a host, it quickly burrows into the skin.

The tiny worm then makes an amazing journey. It finds a vein and catches a ride in the bloodstream. Eventually it reaches a lung. It burrows out of the blood vessel and into one of the lung's air sacs. From there it is coughed up in mucus and swallowed back down into the stomach. Finally, the worm grasps the lining of the small intestine and begins feeding. Five weeks after the original infection, the worm reaches maturity in the intestine. Male and female worms mate and begin producing eggs. Adult hookworms can live for about two years.

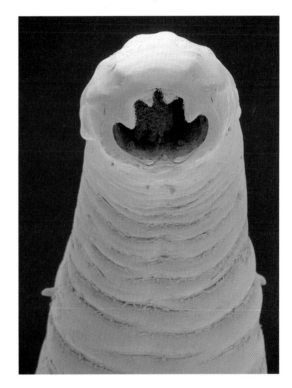

Hookworms use sharp, toothlike structures to latch on to their hosts' intestines.

A severe hookworm infection causes malnutrition and even death. Sufferers become anemic and have little energy. The worms stunt children's growth and cause mental retardation. Hookworms are probably responsible for much of the "laziness" often attributed to people living in warm climates. Hookworms can be treated with drugs, but improved sanitation is the best way to prevent this infection.

Filarial worms

Filarial worms got their name because they are thin like a filament, or thread. The heartworm that can harm pet dogs is a member of this group of nematodes. Many filarial worms are transmitted by biting flies or mosquitoes.

Millions of people suffer from various forms of filariasis (infection by filarial worms). The worm *Wuchereria bancrofti* is the most widespread. It plagues more than one hundred million people in tropical and semitropical regions.

Adult *W. bancrofti* live coiled in the human lymphatic system—the vessels in the body that circulate lymph. Male *W. bancrofti* are about 1.5 inches (4 cm) long. Females grow to almost 4 inches (10 cm). Adult females produce thousands of microscopic young called microfilariae that travel in the bloodstream. Where in the body microfilariae are found depends on the time of day. During daylight hours, the tiny worms migrate to the interior of the body. Blood samples taken from an infected person during that time show few, if any, worms. At night the larvae travel to blood vessels near the skin's surface. This allows mosquitoes that feed at night to transmit the worms to other hosts.

The human immune system reacts to the worms, causing sudden fevers and damaging the lymphatic system. Over time,

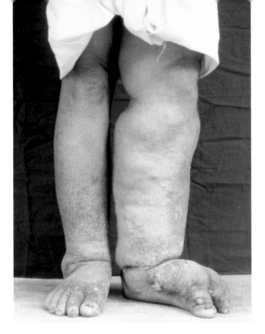

The severe swelling of this man's legs and feet is the result of a filarial worm infection. His condition is called elephantiasis.

the infection can create massive swelling, especially of legs, arms, and sex organs. These swellings give the affliction its common name, elephantiasis.

W. bancrofti infection can be treated with drugs. People can prevent infection by using insect repellent and mosquito netting. Controlling the mosquito population also helps reduce the number of cases of elephantiasis, as well as other mosquito-borne illnesses.

Many other nematodes, spread by poor sanitation or biting insects, infect huge numbers of people in the tropics. *Ascaris lumbricoides*, an intestinal roundworm, infects about 1.3 billion people worldwide. More than 1 billion are infected with whipworms (*Trichuris trichiura*). About 18 million people are afflicted with river blindness, caused by a nematode spread by blackflies. And another 13 million are infected with *Loa loa*. This parasite is spread by several species of deerflies. *Loa loa* is also known as eyeworm, because it sometimes travels just under the surface of the eye.

Chapter Six

ARTHROPOD PARASITES

Arthropods are jointed-legged creatures with a stiff exoskeleton (hard outer covering). They include insects, spiders, centipedes, crustaceans, and several other groups. Arthropods dominate the animal world. There are a million or more different species of arthropods, far more than any other animal phylum. Many thousands of them have evolved to live as parasites.

PARASITIC WASPS

In a backyard garden, a tomato hornworm almost as big as your thumb munches along the underside of a tomato leaf. But this beautiful green caterpillar will never develop into an adult moth. Clinging to its sides are several dozen small, white cocoons. Inside each cocoon is a developing wasp. Two weeks ago, a tiny parasitic wasp deposited her eggs inside the caterpillar's body. The wasp larvae fed on the caterpillar's internal organs. The caterpillar was allowed to live, eating to support the parasites inside it. Then the larvae burrowed out of its body and wove their cocoons. As the young wasps develop in their cocoons, the caterpillar stops feeding and slowly dies.

Wise gardeners leave parasitized hornworms on their plants, instead of killing them. The wasps developing inside the cocoons will help control tomato-eating caterpillars later in the season. Some commercial farmers use wasps in their endless battle with insects. Rather than spraying toxic chemicals, they

Braconid wasp larvae burrowed out of this tomato hornworm caterpillar and formed cocoons. The caterpillar will soon die.

release thousands of parasitic wasps as biological pest control.

There are many thousands of species of parasitic wasps. Some attack just one particular kind of insect, while others are less choosy. Biologists classify these insects as parasitoids rather than parasites, because the wasp larvae always kill their hosts in the end.

MITES

You may have heard someone say a scruffy-looking dog was "mangy." Did you know a parasite is responsible for that phrase?

Mange is a parasitic disease. It's caused by several different species of mites—tiny eight-legged creatures related to spiders and ticks. One species of mite, *Sarcoptes scabiei*, infects both humans and domestic animals. These mites burrow into the skin, causing a rash and severe itching. The condition is called mange in animals and scabies in humans. Mange also affects wild animals, including foxes and coyotes.

After hatching from eggs, juvenile scabies mites remain close to the surface of the skin. They mature in about four days.

This is a greatly magnified view of the mite that causes scabies.

After mating, each female burrows beneath the surface of the skin. She tunnels under the skin for about one month, feeding on skin cells and laying eggs. This causes an itchy rash. Often the skin forms crusty patches in reaction to the invasion. The eggs hatch and develop into mature mites in about three weeks.

Scabies mites prefer less hairy parts of the body, such as the ears or face. But untreated infections eventually spread. Animals with serious infections lose patches of hair, resulting in a scruffy, mangy appearance. Scratching opens the skin to bacterial infections. Serious cases of mange can cause an animal's death.

Most of us also harbor small, harmless colonies of facial mites. These tiny creatures live at the base of eyelashes and other facial hair. They feed on dead hair and skin cells. We don't even know they are there, but their eating habits may cost us an eyelash or eyebrow hair every now and then.

Other species of mites live in the feathers and skin of birds. These mites can reproduce in large enough numbers to weaken or kill their hosts. Farmers who raise chickens or other fowl treat their flocks with pesticides to protect them.

Still other mites parasitize insects. One species, *Acarapis woodi*, lives in the breathing tubes of honeybees. The mites weaken the bees, making it difficult for them to fly and gather food. A heavy infestation can kill off an entire hive. These mites are serious agricultural pests, reducing both honey production and crop pollination. A less common mite, *Varroa destructor*, sucks the blood of honeybees, making it difficult for them to gather enough nectar to survive. From Asia it has spread to most of the world's regions. It is considered the most destructive of all honeybee parasites.

Ticks, mites' larger eight-legged relatives, are bloodsucking parasites that wait in shrubs or grass for a passing vertebrate host. Most ticks need three blood meals during their life cycle. Some spend their entire lives on a single host. Others drop off after feeding and must later find a new host. Some species live for as long as twenty years. Ticks can transmit human diseases including Lyme disease and Rocky Mountain spotted fever.

LICE AND FLEAS

Lice and fleas are insects that suck the blood of birds and mammals, including humans. Humans host several species of lice including *Pediculus humanus*, the head and body louse, and *Phthirus pubis*, the crab louse. People have lived with lice for so long that they have become part of everyday speech. For example, *nit-picking* originally meant carefully removing louse eggs

Above: *Human hairs covered with
louse eggs.* Right: *An electron
micrograph image of a head louse.
At the left, you can see an egg
glued to a strand of hair.*

(nits) from someone's hair. Children often tease one another by
saying someone has "cooties," a slang term for lice. And, of
course, when we don't like something we say it's "lousy."

Head lice and crab lice are about 0.06 inch (less than 2 mm)
long. Body lice can be about twice as large. A female louse lives
about one month, during which time she lays as many as three
hundred eggs. Crab lice and head lice use a gluelike secretion to attach their eggs to the host's hair. Body lice usually lay their eggs in
clothing. The nits hatch in about a week's time. In eight or nine
more days, the insects develop into bloodsucking adults. Lice are
transmitted from one host to another by physical contact or by
sharing combs, brushes, or clothing. Although people in our society may feel embarrassed by an infestation, anyone can get lice.

Lice feed with a tubelike mouth that pierces the skin to reach
a tiny blood vessel. The bite causes redness and itching. But lice
can cause more serious problems than just an itch. Among the

diseases they can transmit is typhus. Typhus killed millions of people before antibiotic drugs such as penicillin were developed.

Fleas have been responsible for even more human destruction. The bite of an infected rat flea, *Xenopsylla cheopi,* can transmit bubonic plague—the black death. Plague wiped out a quarter of the population of Europe in the Middle Ages. Although it can be treated with antibiotics, bubonic plague is still an occasional health threat in the modern world.

About two thousand different species of fleas parasitize birds and mammals, including house pets and humans. Fleas can also be vectors for other parasites, including tapeworms and filarial worms. Fleas stab their host with a feeding tube and drink blood. They lay their eggs loosely in the host's hair, but the eggs drop off. The young fleas often grow up in the host's nest or den. Flea eggs hatch into white, wormlike larvae that metamorphose into pupae. They develop into new adults in about three to four weeks. During cold weather or other unfavorable conditions, fleas can survive as larvae or pupae for almost one year.

Fleas don't have wings, but they are world-champion jumpers. A flea can jump one hundred times its body length. That would be the equivalent of your jumping over a fifty-story building. Obviously, fleas have little trouble catching a ride on a host.

PARASITIC ANTS

We usually think of ants as busy, hardworking insects. You might be surprised to learn that over two hundred kinds of ants live as parasites. One species, *Protomognathus americanus,* turns other ants into slaves.

A newly mature queen ant takes a single mating flight. After she mates, the queen loses her wings and starts a new colony.

*These red ants (*Polyergus*) have enslaved the silver ants (*Formica argentea*) to raise their young.*

The *P. americanus* queen finds a nest of her host species. She attacks the nest and chases its queen and workers away. The *P. americanus* queen then "adopts" the larvae and pupae they leave behind. When they mature, these ants serve their new mistress, even though she is a different species. They care for her eggs and larvae, forage for food, build the nest, and keep it clean. The parasitic queen's offspring don't work at all. They just groom one another and eat food brought to them by their slaves.

The pampered *P. americanus* workers are warriors, however. When the colony needs more slaves, they raid a nearby colony of their host species to steal more larvae and pupae. These juvenile ants also grow up to serve their enslaving mistress.

Other ant species take parasitism even further. They produce no workers at all. *Teleutomyrmex schneideri* is a European parasitic ant. The *T. schneideri* queen uses chemical camouflage to sneak into the nest of a host species. She releases scents that are very attractive to the host workers. The tiny *T. schneideri* queen grasps the body of the larger host queen, and that is where she stays. Host workers feed and care for her and her offspring. New *T. schneideri* queens mate in their host's nest. They either stay in the nest or fly off to find another colony.

Ants themselves are hosts to fungi, protists, mites, flies, beetles, and worms of all sorts. Parasites of ants are so common that this group of creatures has its own name: ant guests, or myrmecophiles (literally, "ant lovers").

The threat of parasites explains one very specialized and puzzling ant behavior. Leafcutter ants harvest leaves, which they carry back to their underground nests. The ants use the leaves to grow a special fungus that feeds the colony. Worker ants carrying pieces of leaf back to the nest often have smaller workers riding on their leaves. Biologists used to think these tiny riders were cleaning the leaves. But it turns out that the smaller workers are actually "riding shotgun."

Small leafcutter workers ride on a leaf piece carried by a larger worker. Their job is to protect the larger ant from parasitic flies.

Parasitic flies hover over the column of ants, waiting for the chance to lay an egg on a worker. If a fly succeeds, the egg hatches into a larva that consumes the worker ant from the inside, eventually killing her. The larger worker is carrying a leaf in her jaws. She has no way to defend herself. So the smaller worker's job is to chase away any fly that tries to attack her big sister.

INSECT PARASITES OF PLANTS

Are the many insects that feed on farm and garden crops parasites? Or are they grazers, like tiny sheep or cows? Many thousands of plant-eating insect species fit the definition of a parasite. They live on or in another organism and get their nutrients from it.

Aphids are a perfect example of an insect that parasitizes plants. Some of these small, soft-bodied insects suck juices from the tender growing tips of many different plants. Other aphids live underground and suck the juices from plant roots. Because of their feeding habits, aphids are sometimes called plant lice.

Aphids and related insects spend their entire lives as parasites. They damage plants by stealing water and nutrients from them and by infecting them with viruses. The leaves of garden plants infested with aphids wilt, curl, or turn yellow. Aphids cost growers millions of dollars in damages each year.

Like many parasites, aphids succeed by reproducing rapidly. Most aphid species produce no males through the growing season. Female aphids give birth to wingless nymphs that are also female. The tiny nymphs begin feeding immediately. In less than two weeks, they mature and produce offspring of their own. In just a few weeks, a population of aphids can explode. At the end of the growing season, aphids lay special eggs that can survive through the winter. Some species produce a generation of male and female aphids that mate to generate the winter eggs. Other species never produce any males at all.

When you find a plant infested with aphids, you will probably find ants too. Aphids are almost defenseless. But they produce a sweet, sticky substance called honeydew that ants love to eat. In return for the food, the ants act as shepherds. They protect the aphids from predators and move them from plant to plant to find the best feeding sites.

Ants care for small, green aphids, protecting them from predators. The ants eat the honeydew that the aphids produce.

SACCULINA

Most barnacles are small sea creatures that cement their shells to rocks or other hard surfaces. Because of their shells, barnacles might seem to be related to clams or oysters. But they are actually crustaceans, relatives of shrimp and crabs. They feed by filtering small food particles out of the water with their legs.

One barnacle lives a fascinating parasitic life. In some ways, *Sacculina carcini* is the ultimate parasite. It has no mouth or digestive system, no nervous system, and no sense organs. As an adult, it is little more than a reproductive system and a mass of rootlike tissues that spread throughout its host.

Sacculina parasitizes crabs. Like any other barnacle, it starts out life as a microscopic swimming larva. But when *Sacculina* is ready to mature, it must find a crab. A female larva finds a joint in a crab's shell and injects a clump of its cells into the crab's body. The parasitic blob travels to the crab's abdomen and begins to grow, sending out "roots" throughout the crab's body. Eventually the parasite produces a huge reproductive organ that bulges from the crab's abdomen. Tiny male *Sacculina* larvae swim into the female parasite's reproductive organ to fertilize her eggs.

Meanwhile the crab has been completely taken over. It continues feeding and supplying nutrients for the parasite. But *Sacculina* prevents the crab from becoming sexually mature. Male crabs infected with *Sacculina* grow to resemble females. They carry the parasite's egg mass just as a female crab would carry her own eggs. The crab protects and cares for the parasite's eggs as if they were its own.

Sacculina was once used as a prime example of how "degenerate" parasites are. After all, it's nothing but a reproductive

This crab has been parasitized by a Sacculina carcini *barnacle. The crab is carrying its parasite's egg mass under its body.*

system and fleshy tentacles that rob its host of nutrients. It's hard not to think of it as a creepy, alien being. But modern biologists hold *Sacculina* and other parasites in higher esteem. This animal is highly specialized. It doesn't *need* legs or eyes or a digestive tract. *Sacculina* has evolved a perfect way to grow and reproduce—all at the expense of its helpless host.

Chapter Seven

VERTEBRATE PARASITES

Most vertebrates—fish, amphibians, reptiles, birds, and mammals—are free-living creatures. They serve as hosts to parasites of all sorts, but only a very few vertebrates live as parasites themselves. Those few—including cuckoos, cowbirds, and lampreys—lead fascinating lives.

CUCKOOS AND COWBIRDS

In a British marsh, a pair of reed warblers carefully constructs a nest. After several days, the female warbler begins laying her eggs. Meanwhile, a cuckoo perches nearby, watching and waiting. One afternoon, when the warblers leave the nest to feed, the cuckoo swoops down. She lays one egg and quickly flies away with one of the warblers' eggs in her beak. Amazingly, the cuckoo completes her visit to the warblers' nest in less than ten seconds. Later, she will eat the stolen egg.

When the warblers return, the female inspects her clutch of eggs carefully. One egg is slightly larger, although its greenish color matches the others. At this point, the warbler may push the foreign egg out of her nest or abandon her eggs altogether. But usually the mother bird is fooled. She accepts the cuckoo's egg as one of her own. Her own chicks are then doomed.

About seventy-five species of cuckoos are brood parasites. They steal parental care from other species. These birds lay their eggs in the nests of other birds and rely on the host birds to feed and raise their young. Parasitic cuckoos live throughout

A Marico sunbird (right) *has been fooled into treating a cuckoo's offspring* (left) *as its own.*

Europe, Asia, and Africa. The familiar cuckoo clock imitates the call of the male common cuckoo, *Cuculus canorus*.

Cuckoos are selective in their choice of host. Different varieties of cuckoos specialize in parasitizing particular species. To help fool the foster parents, the cuckoos' eggs mimic the color and markings of the eggs of their hosts.

Cuckoo eggs are unusually small—just slightly larger than those of their hosts. Most birds the size of a cuckoo lay much larger eggs. During a single breeding season, a female cuckoo lays up to twenty-five eggs in twenty-five different nests.

Cuckoos must be fast to fool their hosts into accepting their eggs. If a cuckoo stays on the host nest too long, its owners chase her away. Timing is also important. Birds ordinarily lay one egg a day, usually in the morning. An experiment by researchers Nicholas Davies and Michael Brooke found that a host bird will reject an egg placed in her nest before she has laid her own. So the cuckoo lays her eggs in the afternoon. Birds can't count. As long as there's at least one of her own eggs in the nest, the host bird seems satisfied. She allows the extra egg to stay.

A young cuckoo incubates quickly and usually hatches before its foster siblings. The young cuckoo is much larger than the host species' chicks. It pushes unhatched eggs and hatchlings out of the nest. It opens its huge mouth wide, stimulating the parents to gather even more food than they would need if they were feeding their own young.

Cowbirds, members of the blackbird family, are brood parasites native to the Americas. Their name comes from their feeding habits. Cowbirds follow bison, cattle, and other large animals. They feed on the insects stirred up as the herd moves through the grass. *Molothrus ater*, the brownheaded cowbird, is common across temperate North America. Several other species of cowbirds live in Central and South America.

A cowbird's migratory life is not well suited to raising young. So the bird has evolved a way to let others do the job. Brownheaded cowbirds parasitize over two hundred different kinds of birds. Some species, such as catbirds and robins, often reject cowbird eggs. But many others accept the eggs easily.

A female cowbird lays a single egg in another bird's nest. Before she lays her egg, the cowbird approaches the nest and offers a preening display. She bows her head and fluffs her feathers, inviting the potential host to groom her. This behavior may relax the host's defenses. The cowbird lays her egg later, while the host is away from her nest.

Cowbird chicks are usually larger than their nest mates. They demand a larger share of the food their foster parents bring. As a result, the hosts' own chicks often starve while the young cowbird thrives.

LAMPREYS

If fish have nightmares, they surely dream of lampreys. Lampreys are a group of eel-like parasitic fish. Like sharks and rays, lampreys have no bones. Their skeletons are made of cartilage. Lampreys also have no jaws. Their mouth is a round sucking disk studded with sharp teeth. Adult lampreys attach their mouths to fish, use their rough tongue to scrape open a wound, and drink blood and body fluids. Lampreys' saliva

The mouth of a sea lamprey reveals the sharp teeth it uses to attach to its host.

contains chemicals that prevent the wound from closing. Where lampreys are common, a single host fish may have several lampreys attached to it at one time. If a fish is attacked often enough, it can become too weak to survive.

Lampreys live in both saltwater and freshwater habitats around the world. The best-known species is *Petromyzon marinus*, the sea lamprey. In the 1950s, these parasites threatened to destroy the Great Lakes fishing industry. Sea lampreys are not native to the upper Great Lakes. But by the 1950s, they had found their way through canals into Lakes Michigan, Huron, and Superior. Their huge numbers almost wiped out the lake trout population and seriously reduced several other species, including whitefish and rainbow trout.

Like salmon, sea lampreys ordinarily spend their adult lives in the ocean, but return to freshwater rivers and streams to spawn. In spring the lampreys swim upstream. The male digs a nest in the river gravel, where the female deposits up to sixty thousand eggs. And like salmon, lampreys die after they spawn.

In about two weeks, tiny wormlike larvae hatch out of the eggs. These blind, toothless creatures live very differently from their parents. They bury themselves tail first in the river bottom. The larvae feed by filtering microscopic organisms out of the water. This larval stage can last for as long as seventeen years.

When the larvae have grown to about 6 inches (15 cm) long, they metamorphose into juvenile lampreys. Over several months, the young parasites develop eyes and round, toothed mouths. Then the young lampreys leave their burrows. They swim downstream in search of their first host.

In rivers, lakes, and the ocean, lampreys locate their hosts by sight. They may use other senses as well. The lamprey opens its mouth and clamps itself to the fish with its sharp teeth.

Lampreys remain attached for an average of three days. Juveniles may hold on for a week or more.

Lampreys seem to prefer certain species of fish, such as lake trout. But they are not fussy. In one study, all seventy-four different species of fish living in an Ohio lake showed evidence of lamprey attacks. Lampreys can swim very fast for short distances. Biologists have found them attached to fast-swimming fish such as sharks and tuna. Lampreys even attack whales.

The sea lamprey lives as a parasite for one or two years. It grows to a length of about 18 inches (45 cm). Mature lampreys then swim upstream to spawn and start the life cycle all over again.

Lampreys are not villains. They are an important part of their native ecosystems. But when they invade a new habitat, such as the Great Lakes, they can cause serious problems.

Fishery scientists eventually found ways to control the sea lamprey. One method is to block their migrations with barriers or electrical shock devices. Biologists also discovered chemicals that kill lamprey larvae without harming other fish. The streams that flow into the Great Lakes are treated with these chemicals every few years. As a result, fish populations in the Great Lakes have recovered almost completely from the lamprey threat.

Chapter Eight

DO PARASITES RULE THE WORLD?

A great egret stands in the shallows of a California marsh, stalking its next meal. The majestic white bird lifts one foot slowly and takes a deliberate step. A silvery flash in the water catches the bird's eye. Its yellow bill stabs the water. The egret tilts its head back, and a little fish slides down its throat. The egret has just swallowed a living package of parasites. The worms in the fish's brain have turned it into easy prey so they could be delivered to the bird, their definitive host.

In order to survive, parasites must move from host to host. To improve their odds of survival, most parasites produce large numbers of offspring. The more young a parasite brings forth, the more likely at least a few of them will find their way to the next host. A pair of schistosomes may produce more than ten million eggs during their lifetime. Some tapeworms produce one million eggs a day!

Parasitologists have discovered other ways that parasites ensure their survival. To make sure they get to their next host, some parasites change their hosts' appearance. Others even control their hosts' behavior.

PARASITES IN CONTROL

Early evidence that parasites control their hosts was discovered in the 1930s. U.S. Department of Agriculture researcher Eloise Cram was studying a nematode that parasitizes chickens. As a larva, this worm lives in grasshoppers. But to reproduce, it must find a bird to be its definitive host. Cram found that the larvae create cysts in the insects' muscles. Grasshoppers infected with the worms can't move as easily as uninfected grasshoppers, so they become much easier for chickens to catch.

Since then, researchers have found many more examples of parasites controlling their hosts' behavior in order to complete their life cycles. Even organisms as simple as fungi have evolved ways to affect their hosts' behavior.

Pillbugs ordinarily stay hidden in the dark, under damp, rotting logs or leaves. But pillbugs infected with *Plagiorhyncus cylindraceus*, a species of parasitic thorny-headed worm, behave differently. Researcher Janice Moore discovered they are much more likely to crawl actively in dry, unprotected areas. Infected pillbugs also choose light-colored background surfaces, where their dark color makes them stand out. Healthy pillbugs never act this way.

The definitive hosts for this particular worm are songbirds, especially starlings. The behavior of the infected pillbugs makes them much easier for birds to see and catch. Starlings don't ordinarily eat many pillbugs. But Moore showed that the birds were much more likely to eat infected pillbugs and infect themselves or their chicks with the worm. This particular parasite isn't just waiting to be eaten. It changes the pillbugs' behavior to improve its chance of reaching its next host.

Flukes are especially expert at controlling their hosts. Some of these flatworms change their intermediate host's appearance, size, or color, making them easy targets for predators. For example, some species of coral are the intermediate host for the fluke *Podocotyloides stenometra*. The infected coral polyps swell and can no longer pull themselves back into their protective stony cup. The polyps also turn bright pink, instead of their ordinary dull brown color. They become attractive prey for butterfly fish, the definitive host of the worm.

Another fluke makes its adult home in birds. Its intermediate host is a snail. The flukes gather in the snail's antennae. The antennae swell until they look like juicy striped caterpillars. What bird could resist?

Dicrocoelium dendriticum, the lancet fluke, reaches its final host by controlling the behavior of ants. This worm's definitive

This coral is infected with a fluke that makes its polyps swell and turn pink, making them attractive prey for the fluke's definitive host.

host is a sheep, cow, or other grazing animal. A snail picks up the fluke's eggs from the animal's manure. The eggs hatch inside the snail. The worm larvae make their way to the snail's digestive system. The snail soon sheds the larvae inside little balls of slime. Each slime ball contains as many as five hundred larvae. An ant finds the slime and eats it. The ant is now infected.

Here's where the story becomes astounding. Fluke larvae make their way to the ant's tiny brain and take control. Somehow the larvae force the ant to act in a way that it never would otherwise. In the evening, instead of returning to its nest, the ant climbs a blade of grass. It grabs the grass with its jaws and holds on. Why?

The flukes need to get into a sheep's stomach to complete their life cycle. When a sheep or some other grazing animal eats the ant along with a mouthful of grass, it gets a bellyful of worms. What if the ant isn't eaten? The next morning, it crawls back down and goes about its business. But that evening, the worms take over and it climbs up another blade of grass to try again.

Killifish are small, minnowlike fish that live in salt marshes. They are one of two intermediate hosts for another species of fluke, *Euhaplorchis californiensis*. This worm's definitive hosts are a variety of different shorebirds. The flukes must get into the birds' digestive systems in order to reproduce.

The worms' eggs pass out in the birds' droppings. They are picked up by marsh snails. The worm larvae develop in the snails, which are then eaten by killifish. The larvae form cysts in the fish's skulls. The parasites then take control of the fish's behavior.

Infected killifish do things that other killifish don't. They swim up to the surface of the water. They flip on their sides, showing their bright white underbellies. They wiggle, shimmy, and jerk. Infected fish are much more obvious to predators.

Some parasites act on a host's behavior to travel between intermediate and definitive hosts. A killifish (above) infected by flukes exposes itself to bird predators, the flukes' definitive hosts.

The more parasites a fish has, the more unusual its behavior seems to become.

Researcher Kevin Lafferty did an experiment to find out if this change in behavior actually helps the parasite reach its final host. He and his colleagues built a pen of netting in the marsh. The pen was open to predatory birds, but the fish could not escape. They put about two hundred killifish in the pen. Half were infected with parasites, and half were not. After twenty days, only a couple of the uninfected fish had been eaten. But half of the infected fish were gone. It turns out that the parasite makes a fish about thirty times as likely to be eaten. Scientists do not yet know just how the worms affect their hosts' behavior. But clearly this parasitic worm is not just waiting to be eaten.

PARASITES IN THE FOOD WEB

We know parasites affect the behavior of their hosts. That discovery forces us to look at the food web in a new way. We know predators such as cougars, foxes, and wolves select weak or injured animals as prey. This helps keep an ecosystem in balance. By killing sick animals, predators regulate the numbers of grazing animals in an ecosystem and help keep their populations healthier.

But those weakened prey may have been weakened by parasites such as flukes, *Trichinella*, or tapeworms. The parasites need to reach a predator to complete their life cycle. If they disable a deer or rabbit, they improve their chances of being eaten by a predator.

For example, the larvae of one tapeworm species, *Taenia multiceps*, invade the brain and spinal cord of sheep, causing a disease called gid. Infected sheep stumble and wander in circles. Their behavior makes it much easier for wild dogs and wolves to separate them from the herd and kill them. Dogs and wolves are the worms' definitive hosts. The worms can reproduce only inside the predators' intestines. The parasite controls the sheep's behavior so it can infect its final host.

We often think of predators as the dominant creatures in any habitat. But maybe they're not. Perhaps the parasites are the organisms in control. Parasites hiding unnoticed inside other creatures have at least some control over who eats—and who gets eaten—in an ecosystem. Parasitology shows us that the natural world is much more complex than it might look.

Chapter Nine

EVOLUTION OF PARASITES

The parasitic life has some obvious advantages. Parasites always have a place to live. They never have to search for food, because they're surrounded by it. Often the host's body provides warmth and protection as well.

Of course, there are disadvantages too. Hosts' immune systems often evict invading parasites. Parasites can't easily move if their living "home" is damaged or destroyed. And parasites are so dependent on their hosts that without them, they die. Nevertheless, the advantages surely outweigh the disadvantages. Otherwise our world wouldn't have so many parasitic species.

Parasites have probably lived on Earth for almost as long as life itself. The different groups of parasites you've met in this book are not closely related at all. One group did not inherit its parasitic way of life from another. Plants, fungi, protozoa, worms, arthropods, and vertebrates evolved parasitic lives independently at many different times during Earth's history.

WHAT IS EVOLUTION?

All species evolve. That means they adapt, or change, to better take advantage of their environment. As the environment changes, species must either adapt to those changes or become extinct. Success in evolution simply means surviving long enough to produce offspring.

This illustration made by British naturalist Charles Darwin shows that four different finch species evolved four distinct beak shapes to fit the different food sources in their individual habitats.

Each individual creature passes on a copy of its genetic code—its DNA (deoxyribonucleic acid)—to its offspring. DNA is a molecule shaped like a spiral ladder. It is made up of segments called genes. Genes determine all inherited traits, such as eye color. An organism's DNA contains all the information needed for an individual of that species to grow. Mating mixes the slightly different genetic information offspring receive from each parent.

Each individual is slightly different. And some variations give a creature a better chance of survival. Individuals with traits that help them survive are more likely to have offspring. So they are more likely to pass their genes on to the next generation. As the most successful variations get passed on, a species gradually evolves over many thousands of generations.

Sometimes genes mutate, or change quickly. A chemical reaction, a virus, or a stray bit of radiation may change the information in the genetic code. Sometimes mutations occur because genes are not copied correctly when a creature reproduces.

Usually mutations don't make much difference. Sometimes they handicap the offspring, causing it to have too few legs or weaker muscles, for example. In that case, the offspring is likely to die before it produces offspring of its own. The harmful change dies with it.

Every now and then, a variation in the DNA produces a useful trait—one that provides an advantage. The change may produce coloration that helps an individual avoid predators. Or it may produce a wider jaw that enables the creature to grasp more food. If a new trait helps it survive longer, the individual is more likely to produce offspring of its own.

Over many generations, useful traits are passed to more and more offspring. They become adaptations. Meanwhile, changes that are not useful for survival die out. Through this process, a species gradually evolves.

Evolution takes place over many, many generations. This usually requires very long periods of time. However, some creatures, including single-celled organisms, reproduce rapidly. They go through thousands of generations in just a few years. This allows them to evolve rapidly.

Scientists have seen parasites evolving. In the past half-century, for example, *Plasmodium falciparum*, the most deadly malaria parasite, has evolved resistance to many antimalarial drugs. Drugs that once controlled the parasite no longer work. The trypanosome that causes nagana has also evolved resistance to a drug that was once used to treat that disease.

BECOMING PARASITIC

Scientists have never seen a free-living creature evolve into a parasite. But it's not hard to imagine how it could happen. Some creatures may have become parasites when their eggs or larvae were accidentally eaten by potential hosts. Perhaps others were injected into potential hosts' bodies with the bite of an insect or other animal. Still others may have entered potential hosts through the skin while looking for a meal or a place to breed.

Here's one imaginary scenario. Some flies lay their eggs on dead animal carcasses. The larvae feed on the rotting meat. Imagine that a few of these flies land on an animal that is ill, but not yet dead. Perhaps their genes have programmed them to lay eggs on an animal that is still warm. The flies deposit their eggs under the animal's skin. But instead of dying, the animal recovers. It gets up and walks away. Meanwhile, the eggs hatch and the larvae begin to feed.

Let's suppose that the living animal provides nutritious food that suits the larvae. The larvae can develop without being disturbed. Unlike a corpse, the living animal can defend itself from creatures that might tear into its flesh, destroying the fly larvae in the process.

So the larvae feed, grow, and eventually develop into new flies. They carry the genes they inherited from their parents. So they too will be more likely to land on a living animal instead of a dead one. If this behavior improves their chance for survival, more and more of these flies will live to maturity, mate, and produce offspring. Eventually, over many generations, a new species of parasitic fly will evolve from its carrion-breeding ancestor.

Such parasitic botflies actually exist in some parts of the world. But remember, this is just a story. No one knows exactly how those flies actually evolved.

Through evolution, parasites also lose body structures they no longer need for survival. For example, the ancestors of lice had wings, like most other insects. But wings are useless for a life spent clinging to an animal's hair or feathers. So over many generations, lice lost this trait. Similarly, ancient ancestors of tapeworms must have had digestive systems. But inside the intestine of another animal, a digestive tract is unnecessary. Modern-day tapeworms have evolved to live without any digestive organs. They just absorb nutrients from their environment.

HOSTS AND PARASITES EVOLVE TOGETHER

Organisms adapt to their environment. In a parasite's case, the host is its environment. But host species also evolve. And parasites are part of *their* environment. So over time, parasites and hosts evolve in response to one another. Parasites evolve to take advantage of their hosts. Hosts evolve defenses against parasites. A change in one species results in a corresponding change in the other. This evolutionary back-and-forth is known as coevolution.

Many hosts, including all mammals, have complex immune systems. These immune systems evolved, at least in part, to respond to parasitic attacks. Individuals with the best immune systems are most likely to survive long enough to pass their genes—including those that create the immune system—on to their offspring.

Parasites and their hosts are in a never-ending evolutionary "arms race." A host evolves a better way to fight off a parasite. The parasite responds by evolving more effective ways of overcoming the host's defenses. The host then evolves a new resistant trait and so on. And after all this change, neither the parasite species nor the host species is any better off than before.

Biologists call this the Red Queen's race, after the character in Lewis Carroll's *Through the Looking Glass*. Alice discovers she is running without getting anywhere. The Red Queen answers that in her kingdom "it takes all the running you can do to keep in the same place." Although it doesn't seem to go anywhere, this endless arms race between parasites and hosts pushes species to continue evolving.

Sickle-Cell Anemia and Malaria

Many people harbor living evidence that our own species has evolved to fight parasites. People of African descent often have a genetic characteristic called sickle-cell trait. Some people of Mediterranean descent carry a similar gene. If a child inherits two copies of the sickle-cell gene—one from each parent—he or she develops a condition called sickle-cell anemia. The blood cannot circulate effectively or carry enough oxygen. This weakens the child and usually results in a shortened life span.

Over generations, you would expect this trait to die out. People who carry it would be less likely to have healthy children who could eventually pass on their genes. But instead, the sickle-cell trait is very common. Almost 10 percent of African Americans carry it. Why?

Inheriting a copy of this gene from only one parent gives a child resistance to malaria. The gene produces a defective form of hemoglobin, the chemical in red blood cells that carries oxygen. The defective hemoglobin makes it hard for *Plasmodium* to survive. So the trait carries a great benefit for people in malaria-infested areas.

A child who inherits only one copy of the sickle-cell gene has a survival advantage. The child can better fight off malaria. So individuals with the trait are more likely to survive and pass that trait to their own children. The trait helps about twice as many children as it harms, so it continues to be passed from generation to generation.

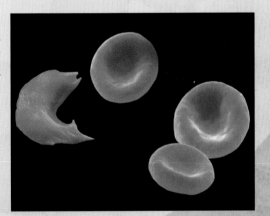

A defective sickle-shaped red blood cell (left) *with three normal cells.*

A male ruffed grouse fans his tail and puffs up his neck feathers to attract a mate. Courtship displays may help female birds choose relatively parasite-free mates.

Some scientists think parasites may even be partly responsible for the evolution of sex. From a practical point of view, sexual reproduction is wasteful. It requires two individuals to reproduce, instead of just one. Half the population—males—fertilize eggs but produce no offspring of their own. Courtship uses energy that could otherwise be applied to feeding or caring for young. Meanwhile, the female does most of the work, producing eggs and raising young. When a female reproduces sexually, she passes on only half of her genes to her offspring. Wouldn't it make more sense for her to do without males altogether? Females could just pass all their genes on to the next generation, as aphids and some other species do.

The advantage of sexual reproduction is that it mixes the genes from two different individuals. Sex creates genetic variation. This mixing allows useful traits, including resistance to parasites, to spread through a population.

It turns out that some females do choose their mates based on their resistance to parasites. Experiments with birds show that sexual displays such as bright colors, fancy plumage, and complicated mating rituals help females select relatively parasite-free mates. The males with the best displays—and fewest parasites—get chosen. Their resistance then gets passed along to the next generation.

EVOLUTION AND VIRULENCE

Another result of coevolution is the tendency for some parasites to become less virulent over time. A parasite depends on its host to live. If it kills its host before it has time to reproduce, a parasite is destroying itself as well. A parasite that keeps its host alive longer ought to be able to produce more offspring. Therefore, you might expect a "gentler" parasite to have an advantage. Over many generations, parasites often evolve to become less virulent.

This isn't always true, however. Parasites that produce large numbers of offspring quickly often remain more harmful to their hosts. Having many offspring makes it more likely that a parasite will reproduce successfully. But it is usually much harder on the host. In such cases, the process of evolution favors greater virulence, especially when it's easy for the parasite to find new hosts. Parasites that thrive where hosts live in crowded conditions tend to be more virulent. If the parasite kills its host quickly, it can easily find new hosts.

Dr. Paul Ewald has noted several other rules that seem to govern the virulence of parasites. For example, vector-borne parasites tend to be more virulent than those passed directly from one host to another. Vectors such as mosquitoes can transmit a parasite even when the host is too sick to move. On the other hand, parasites transmitted directly from host to host must rely on their host's ability to move around. They can't afford to make their hosts too sick.

Crowded, unsanitary conditions, such as those in this village in the Philippines that lacks indoor plumbing and a waste disposal system, help infection spread through the population.

Vector-borne parasites, such as *Plasmodium* or filarial worms, gain an advantage by producing large numbers of offspring in the host's body. This increases the chance that a biting insect will ingest a large number of parasites when it takes its meal. A population explosion of these parasites in the body makes the host terribly ill. But the parasites don't need a healthy host. A mosquito will take care of transporting them from the infected host to their next victim.

Parasites that are passed from one generation of host to the next—from host parent to host offspring—tend to be less virulent. It wouldn't be an advantage to do their hosts serious harm. The survival of such parasites depends on their hosts' ability to live and reproduce.

Another trend is for parasites to be virulent in intermediate hosts, while doing less damage to the definitive hosts that prey on those intermediate hosts. For example, the tapeworm that

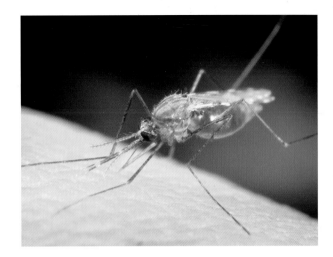

A mosquito draws a blood meal from its human host. If this host's blood is infected with parasites, the mosquito will pass the infection to the next host it bites.

causes gid damages a sheep's ability to escape from predators. The worm increases the chance that the sheep will be caught and eaten. But the worm does little harm to the wild dogs and wolves that are its definitive hosts. It lives in the predators' intestines and produces many eggs while the hosts go about their lives.

Similarly, the *Plasmodium* parasites that are so harmful to their intermediate human hosts do little damage to mosquitoes, their definitive hosts. A feverish, bedridden human is easy prey for a mosquito. But a lively, mobile mosquito helps *Plasmodium* travel to its next human host.

Each species of parasite evolves to a point where its need to reproduce and its need to be transmitted are in balance. The parasite steals as much nutrition from its host as it can. But the parasite cannot do so much damage that its offspring don't get passed on to the next host. This balance point determines whether an infection will be virtually harmless, cause mild disability, or result in terrible misery and death.

Chapter Ten

In the country of Zambia in southern Africa, humans are doing their part to curtail the spread of disease carried by the tsetse fly.

Parasites are one of the great scourges of humankind. They take millions of lives each year. Because infected people are too weak to do their best work or may not be able to work at all, parasites also cost billions of dollars in lost productivity. They cause additional billions of dollars in crop and livestock losses. Almost half the world's farmland cannot be used because it is infested with malaria, trypanosomes, schistosomes, or other parasites.

Parasitic infections are closely associated with poverty. Parasites thrive where people live in crowded housing, with poor sanitation and inadequate nutrition. Where people are densely concentrated, parasites travel easily from one person to another. Poorly nourished people are less able to fight off infections.

Sometimes efforts to improve people's lives can make things worse. For example, dams and irrigation projects allow people to grow more food. But they also produce lakes, ponds, and ditches full of water that breed malaria-spreading mosquitoes and snails that harbor schistosomes.

So how do we defend ourselves against the parasites in our world? Each of us carries our own arsenal in the war against parasites: a highly effective immune system. Our white blood cells and antibodies recognize invaders and destroy them. Some of us have special genetic ammunition, like the sickle-cell trait, that gives us extra protection against certain parasites. But as we've seen, parasites have evolved ways to defeat or hide from our body's defenses. So we must turn to scientific research, medicine, and public health measures to help in the fight.

Public health measures are often the simplest, most effective, and least expensive defense. Digging a new, clean well or teaching basic sanitation techniques can greatly reduce a village's burden of parasites. Draining or spraying pools where mosquitoes breed or spraying bushes where flies rest during the heat of the day can make a big difference in people's lives.

Public health measures may even succeed in conquering a parasite that has plagued humanity since prehistoric times. Guinea worm infections have already been reduced from millions of cases to less than one hundred thousand each year. In many places, public health workers have used water filtration and pesticides to eliminate the tiny shrimplike copepods that carry the juvenile worms. They try to keep infected people away from water sources to prevent more worms from entering the water supply.

This fabric, created by the World Health Organization for its guinea worm eradication project, was used to educate people to filter their water to avoid guinea worm infection. The woman with a baby on her back, a symbol of good health, is correctly filtering her drinking water. The man with a crutch did not filter his water and is suffering from guinea worm infection.

Guinea worm infections may disappear completely within our lifetime. This could be the first time in history that people have eradicated a human parasite from the world. The guinea worm is one species that few people are likely to miss.

We also fight parasites with medical treatment. People have used herbal remedies against parasites for thousands of years. Some animals may also medicate themselves to get rid of parasites. Gorillas and chimpanzees, for example, are known to consume certain bitter leaves when their stomachs are upset. Scientists suspect they do this to help fight off parasites in their digestive system.

The earliest medications for malaria, cinchona and qing-hao, both come from plants. Both of these plants have been used by traditional healers for many hundreds or even thousands of years. Drugs extracted from these plants are still used. Scientists have modified these natural medicines, creating synthetic chemicals that are even more effective. Nevertheless, parasites such as *Plasmodium*, amoebas, and schistosomes have a remarkable ability to adapt to drugs. Drug-resistant strains of these parasites force us to search for new chemical weapons to use against them. It's the parasite–host arms race all over again.

Some parasites can be treated only with drugs that are toxic to humans. The treatment for advanced sleeping sickness, for example, can kill a patient instead of curing him. Researchers are seeking new treatments to control the parasite while doing less harm to the patient.

Drugs that fight parasites can also be expensive. For example, praziquantel can cure schistosomiasis with a single dose, but that dose costs thirty dollars. That's a month's income for some people in Africa and Asia. Bayer, the drug's manufacturer, sells the drug for two dollars per dose to the world's poor nations. But even that is very expensive for a poor family.

Drug companies invest both time and money to create new medications, hoping to earn profits from drug sales. But how much profit can they earn in places where people have little money? Drug manufacturers have little incentive to develop new antiparasitic medicines. They can earn much more by creating new drugs for people in the wealthy developed world instead. So governments must pay for much of the cost of developing drugs to combat parasites. Philanthropic organizations, most notably the Wellcome Trust and the Bill and Melinda Gates Foundation, also spend millions of dollars in support of research to combat parasites.

The third front in the war against parasites is scientific research. Once we understand a parasite's life cycle, we may be able to find ways to interrupt it. That is what allowed William

Gorgas and his colleagues to control malaria and yellow fever in the Panama Canal Zone. They couldn't have succeeded without understanding how those diseases spread. The more we know about a parasite's genes and the proteins that protect it against our immune system, the better our chance of finding ways to control it.

The campaign to develop vaccines is one of the most hopeful areas in the fight against parasites. Vaccines turn on our immune systems in advance. When a vaccine is injected into our body, the immune system creates antibodies that can recognize a particular foreign invader. Then, if the disease organism attacks us, our immune system is ready. It can react immediately and destroy the organism.

Scientists are working on vaccines for malaria and for schistosomiasis. Experimental vaccines to combat both parasites already exist. But so far, the vaccines are not effective enough and their protection doesn't last.

Creating vaccines for these diseases is harder than making one to fight a bacterium or virus. Each of these diseases is caused by several different species of organism. Our immune system reacts to each species differently. In addition, each parasite goes through several different stages of development. Our immune system considers each stage a completely different creature.

Despite these problems, many scientists believe they will soon succeed in making effective vaccines for both malaria and schistosomiasis. But making the vaccines is just half the battle. People must then be immunized. Imagine the monumental task and huge expense of manufacturing enough vaccine and then immunizing the billions of people who live in malaria-infested regions. Many of those people live in remote areas, far from the nearest airfield or paved road. How will health-care

Scientists are trying to find a vaccine for malaria. Such a vaccine could save millions of lives.

workers reach those people? How will they keep the vaccine safe and pure while they do? The project would take many years.

Elimination of parasitic diseases from our world is not a realistic possibility. Parasites are a part of the web of life on Earth. We will never be completely free of them. The best we can do is to limit the number of parasitic infections that plague us and treat people when they do become infected.

Parasites are everywhere in our world. Our strategy in the war against parasites must include learning how to live among them. So don't forget to wash your hands.

MAJOR PARASITES
OF HUMANS

Organism	Estimated number of infections worldwide
Ascaris lumbricoides	1.5 billion
Trichuris trichiura (whipworm)	1.1 billion
Hookworm—various species	1 billion
Enterobius vermicularis (pinworm)	500+ million
Entamoeba histolytica (causes dysentery)	500+ million
Plasmodium—several species (causes malaria)	300 million
Giardia duodenalis (intestinal flagellate)	200 million
Schistosomes (blood flukes)	200 million
Wuchereria bancrofti (causes elephantiasis)	110 million
Taenia saginata and *T. solium* (tapeworms)	90 million
Strongyloides (intestinal nematode worm)	70 million
Onchocerca volvulus (causes river blindness)	20+ million
Liver flukes—various species, including *Fasciola hepatica* and *Clonorchis sinensis*	20 million
Trypanosoma cruzi (causes Chagas disease)	18 million
Loa loa (eyeworm)	13 million
Leishmania—various species (flagellates)	12 million
Diphyllobothrium latum (fish tapeworm)	10 million
Trypanosoma brucei (causes sleeping sickness)	500,000+
Dracunculus medinensis (guinea worm)	80,000

GLOSSARY

amoeba: a single-celled organism that constantly changes its shape

antibiotics: substances that kill or slow the growth of bacteria

arthropods: jointed-legged creatures with a hard outer covering, such as insects, spiders, centipedes, and crustaceans

brood parasites: birds or insects that steal parental care from other species

chlorophyll: the chemical that enables plants to turn water and carbon dioxide into sugars through photosynthesis

coevolution: the process of two species evolving in response to one another

commensalism: a symbiotic relationship in which one creature benefits and the other is neither helped nor harmed

crustacean: an animal with no backbone that has a hard shell and many jointed legs. Crabs, lobsters, and barnacles are crustaceans.

cyst: a thick-walled capsule enclosing an organism's resting stage

definitive host: the species that hosts a parasite's adult, reproductive stage

DNA (deoxyribonucleic acid): the molecule that contains genetic information and is passed from parent to offspring during reproduction

evolve: to change to better take advantage of the environment. Species evolve over many generations.

feces: solid bodily wastes

flagellates: single-celled creatures that use a whiplike structure called a flagellum to propel themselves

fungi: spore-producing organisms that absorb nutrients from other organisms

gene: the basic unit of heredity; a segment of DNA that transmits a hereditary characteristic from parent to offspring

genus (pl. genera): a group of closely related species

germinate: to sprout

haustoria: rootlike growths that parasitic plants and fungi use to absorb food from their hosts

helminth: an animal with no backbone whose body is long and thin; a worm

host: a living plant or animal that provides food and habitat for a parasite

immune system: the complex system that defends the body against disease

intermediate host: a species that hosts a juvenile stage of a parasite

larva: the immature or juvenile form of an animal

lymphatic system: vessels in the body that circulate lymph, a clear body fluid that contains only white blood cells

metamorphosis: the process of changing from one life stage to another

mites: tiny eight-legged creatures related to spiders and ticks

mutualism: a symbiotic relationship in which both partners benefit

nematodes: unsegmented roundworms; some species are parasites

organism: a living creature

parasite: an organism that lives in or on another organism, called the host, and gets its nutrients directly from it

parasitism: a symbiotic relationship in which one organism uses the other for both food and habitat; the host is harmed but usually is not killed

parasitoid: a parasite that kills its host as part of its life cycle

parasitology: the scientific study of parasites

phylum (pl. phyla): a major group of species. The largest animal phylum, Arthropoda, includes one million or more different species.

predation: a symbiotic relationship in which one organism kills and eats the other

protists: single-celled organisms that are neither plants nor animals but that have characteristics of both

protozoan (pl. protozoa): a single-celled animal

pupa (pl. pupae): the resting stage in an insect's life cycle between the larva and the adult

sexual reproduction: a form of reproduction involving two parents, each of which passes genetic material to the offspring

species: a single type of organism, able to reproduce only with others of its own kind

spores: the reproductive cells of fungi, nonflowering plants such as ferns and mosses, and some single-celled organisms

symbiosis: the relationship between two different species that live together and interact with one another

trait: a characteristic of an organism

vaccine: a substance that protects the body from a particular disease

vector: a host, such as a mosquito, that transmits parasites or disease from one organism to another

vertebrates: animals with backbones

virulence: the degree to which a parasite harms its host

zoonosis: a disease that normally occurs only in animals but may also infect humans

SELECTED BIBLIOGRAPHY

Ash, Lawrence R., and Thomas C. Orihel. *Atlas of Human Parasitology*, 4th ed. Chicago: American Society for Clinical Pathology Press, 1997.

Ashford, R. W., and W. Crewe. *The Parasites of Homo sapiens: An Annotated Checklist of the Protozoa, Helminths, and Arthropods for Which We Are Home*. New York: Taylor and Francis, 2003.

De Kruif, Paul. *The Microbe Hunters*. San Diego: Harcourt Brace & Co., 1926.

DeSalle, Rob, ed. *Epidemic!: The World of Infectious Disease*. New York: New Press, 1999.

Desowitz, Robert S. *The Malaria Capers: More Tales of Parasites and People, Research and Reality*. New York: W. W. Norton, 1991.

———. *New Guinea Tapeworms and Jewish Grandmothers: Tales of Parasites and People*. New York: W. W. Norton, 1987.

Ewald, Paul, *Evolution of Infectious Diseases*. Oxford, UK: Oxford University Press, 1994.

Honigsbaum, Mark. *The Fever Trail: In Search of the Cure for Malaria*. New York: Farrar, Straus and Giroux, 2002.

Roueché, Berton. *The Medical Detectives*. New York: Truman Talley Books/Plume, 1988.

Schmidt, Gerald D., and Larry S. Roberts, *Foundations of Parasitology*. 3rd ed. Saint Louis: Times Mirror/Mosby, 1985.

Zimmer, Carl. *Parasite Rex: Inside the Bizarre World of Nature's Most Dangerous Creatures*. New York: Free Press, 2000.

FURTHER READING AND WEBSITES

BOOKS

Doyle, Mycol. *Killer Plants: The Venus Flytrap, Strangler Fig, and Other Predatory Plants.* Los Angeles: Lowell House, 1993.

Facklam, Howard, and Margery Facklam. *Parasites.* New York: Twenty-First Century Books, 1994.

Freidlander, Mark P. *Outbreak: Disease Detectives at Work.* Minneapolis: Lerner Publications Company, 2003.

Freidlander, Mark P., and Terry M. Phillips. *The Immune System: Your Body's Disease-Fighting Army.* Minneapolis, Lerner Publications Company, 2003.

Knutson, Roger. *Fearsome Fauna: A Field Guide to the Creatures That Live in You.* New York: W. H. Freeman, 1999.

Ward, Brian R. *Epidemic.* New York: Dorling Kindersley, 2000.

WEBSITES

Forest Pathology—Parasitic Plants
http://wiww.forestpathology.org/mistle.html
  This site has lots of information on mistletoe, including mistletoe-related folklore.

Parasites and Foodborne Illnesses
http://www.fsis.usda.gov/OA/pubs/parasite.htm
  This site from the U.S. Department of Agriculture provides information on the parasites most likely to be found in food and water in the United States.

Parasites and Health
http://www.dpd.cdc.gov/dpdx/HTML/Para_Health.htm
  This site from the Centers for Disease Control and Prevention (CDC) has detailed information on the life cycles of a wide range of parasites of humans.

Parasites and Parasitological Resources
http://www.biosci.ohio-state.edu/~parasite/home.html
  This site contains a wealth of information, including photos of parasites, diagrams of body parts and life cycles, and answers to common questions about parasites of pets.

INDEX

ABOUT THE AUTHOR

Paul Fleisher has written more than two dozen books for young people and educators on topics including natural history, environmental science, technology, the nuclear arms race, writing, and educational games. He also writes commentary and reviews computer software. Fleisher taught gifted elementary and middle school students in the Richmond, Virginia, public schools for more than twenty-five years and continues to teach adult education classes. His books include *The Big Bang, Evolution, Ice Cream Treats: The Inside Scoop, Liquids and Gases, Matter and Energy, Objects in Motion, Relativity and Quantum Mechanics,* and *Waves.*

PHOTO ACKNOWLEDGMENTS

© Dr. Dennis Kunkel/Visuals Unlimited, pp. 1, 46, 48; © Roger Klocek/Visuals Unlimited, p. 2; © Andrew Syred/Photo Researchers, Inc., pp. 6, 26; © Reinhard Dirscherl/Visuals Unlimited, p. 10; U.S. Air Force, p. 13 (main); Centers for Disease Control and Prevention, pp. 25 (left), 38, 55 (both), 56, 97, and background images on pp. 13, 16, 42–43, 52–53, 93; © Bettmann/CORBIS, p. 15; © Andrew J. Martinez/Photo Researchers, Inc., p. 16 (main); © Biodisc/Visuals Unlimited, p. 19; © Dr. C. P. Hickman/Visuals Unlimited, p. 21; © M. F. Brown/Visuals Unlimited, p. 22; © Rob & Ann Simpson/Visuals Unlimited, p. 25 (right); © Ken Wagner/Visuals Unlimited , p. 28; © Inga Spence/Visuals Unlimited, p. 30; © Dayton Wild/Visuals Unlimited, p. 31; © Daniel L. Nickrent and Lytton J. Musselman, p. 33; © Henry Lehn/Visuals Unlimited, p. 35; © Compost/Peter Arnold, p. 37; © Martin Dohrn/Photo Researchers, Inc., p. 40; Diagram artwork by Laura Westlund, pp. 42–43, 52–53; © Sinclair Stammers/Photo Researchers, Inc., p. 50; © John Mason/Ardea, p. 59; © David Scharf/Photo Researchers, Inc., p. 61; © R. Umesh Chandran, TDR, WHO/Photo Researchers, Inc., p. 63; © Jerome Wexler/Visuals Unlimited, p. 65; © Cath Wadforth/Photo Researchers, Inc., p. 66; © St. Bartholomew's Hospital/Photo Researchers, Inc., p. 68 (main); © Mona Lisa Production/Photo Researchers, Inc., p. 68 (inset); © Alex Wild, p. 70; © William Ervin/Photo Researchers, Inc., p. 71; © Ray Coleman/Visuals Unlimited, p. 73; © Heather Angel/Natural Visions, p. 75; © Joe McDonald/Visuals Unlimited, p. 77; © Science VU/Visuals Unlimited, p. 79; © Darlyne A. Murawski/Peter Arnold, Inc., p. 84; © Patrice Ceisel/Visuals Unlimited, p. 86; The Zoological Society of London, p. 89; © Dr. Stanley Flegler/Visuals Unlimited, p. 93 (main); © Gerard Fuehrer/Visuals Unlimited, p. 94; © Mark Edwards/Peter Arnold, Inc., pp. 96, 103; © Ron Giling/Peter Arnold, Inc., p. 98; © Todd Strand/Independent Picture Service, p. 100.

Front cover: © Mona Lisa Production/Photo Researchers Inc. Back cover: Centers for Disease and Control and Prevention Public Health Image Library (all).